FROM CODER TO CTO

The Power of Technical
Blogging in Tech Careers

By Asaf Zamir

Copyright © 2024 by Asaf Zamir All rights reserved.

No part of this book may be reproduced, distributed, or transmitted in any form or by any means, including photocopying, recording, or other electronic or mechanical methods, without the prior written permission of the author, except in the case of brief quotations embodied in critical reviews and certain other noncommercial uses permitted by copyright law. This is a work of non-fiction.

Names, characters, places, and incidents either are products of the author's imagination or are used fictitiously. Any resemblance to actual persons, living or dead, events, or locales is entirely coincidental.

ISBN: 979-8-3376-3876-8

First Edition

I dedicate this book to the three most important girls in my life.

Alma, who will always be my companion in this amazing, spectacular, sometimes crazy journey we call life. You are my source of power. You remind me that we choose to do these things not because they are easy, but because they are hard.

Grace, who has made me a father, and taught me again how to be a child. I see so much of myself in you, you give me hope for the future.

Eleanor, who has made us a family of four. We are so happy you have finally arrived. You help me remember to sometimes take a break and smell the roses.

Table of Contents

Chapter 1: Getting Started with Technical Blogging 1
    What is Technical Blogging? 2
    The Challenges and Rewards of Technical Blogging 3
    Personal Journey: Learning and Sharing AngularJS 5
    The Impact of Technical Blogging on the Tech Community 6
    Case Study: Google Cloud Platform Migration 8
    From Blogging to Career Advancement 10
    Tools and Techniques: Enhancing the Blogging Process 12
    Conclusion 15

Chapter 2: Embracing the Tools of the Trade 17
    Orgmode: A Powerhouse for Organization and Productivity 18
    The Philosophy of Minimalism in Tools 22
    The Power of Open Source 24
    Practical Applications and Contributions 27
    Navigating the Proprietary-Open Source Divide 30
    Conclusion 33

Chapter 3: Crafting Compelling Technical Content 35
    Leveraging and Embracing Cutting-Edge Technologies 36

Overcoming Challenges with Emerging Technologies 42

Keeping Up with Technology Trends 45

The Imperative of Continual Learning 47

Career Advancement Through Continuous Learning and Adaptation 48

Conclusion: The Power of Curiosity and Adaptation 52

Chapter 4: Overcoming Challenges 55

Overcoming Writer's Block 56

Taking a Long Break 59

Deciding to Move to Another Domain 62

Balancing Work and Play During Workations 66

The Unexpected Benefits of Workations 70

Engaging with Readers During Breaks 71

Conclusion: Embracing Challenges as Opportunities for Growth 73

Chapter 5: Growing Your Blog 75

Search Engine Optimization (SEO) for Technical Blogs 76

Leveraging Social Media for Blog Growth 80

Email Marketing for Bloggers 85

Networking and Collaboration in the Tech Blogging Space 89

Engaging with Your Readers 93

Content Distribution Strategies 96

Analytics and Metrics for Blog Growth 98

Building a Personal Brand Through Your Blog 101

Monetization Strategies (While Maintaining Community Focus) .. 104

Scaling Your Blog's Growth 107

Overcoming Growth Plateaus 109

Transforming Community Engagement into
Business Opportunities 112

Measuring Community Engagement 115

Case Studies: Successful Technical Bloggers 117

The Impact of Community Platforms on Technical Blogging 119

Conclusion: The Ongoing Nature of Community Building 120

Chapter 6: The Impact of Blogging on Your Career 123

The Digital Evolution of Professional Networking 123

Blogging as a Learning Tool 125

Blogging as a Career Catalyst 126

A Direct Line to Decision Makers 134

The Power of Sharing Technical Solutions and
Portfolio Building 135

Conclusion: The Transformative Power of Technical
Blogging 137

Chapter 7: My Personal Blogging Journey 139

The Early Days: A Tech News Website in Junior High 139

From PHPNuke to Professional Recognition 140

The WordPress Years and a Bold Move to Germany 141

The Google Grant and a Lesson in Cloud Security 142

Scaling the Career Ladder: From Full Stack Developer
to a Global Tech Lead 143

Pivoting to Leadership: The Journey to CTO 145

    Fractional CTO and Tech Lead: Freelance Freedom 150

    Reflecting on the Impact of Technical Writing 161

    Lessons Learned and Advice for Aspiring Technical Bloggers 162

    Conclusion: The Enduring Power of Technical Blogging 163

Chapter 8: The Future of Technical Blogging 165

    The Future of AI in Blogging 166

    Who Owns the Content? 168

    The SEO Challenge 169

    Will AI Overtake All Blogging? 171

    The Convergence of Immersive Technologies and Blogging 174

    Decentralization: A Returning Phenomenon? 176

    Long-form Content in a Bite-sized World 178

    Navigating the Future Landscape of Content Creation Tools 180

    Conclusion: Embracing the Future of Technical Blogging 181

Final Thoughts: The Blog That Stood the Test of Time 183

Glossary 187

CHAPTER 1

Getting Started with Technical Blogging

Here's something I've learned over the years: in tech, change is the only constant. Tech stacks evolve, frameworks come and go, and what's big today might be obsolete tomorrow. But there's one thing that sticks with you throughout your career - your own record of what you've learned and how you've grown. That's where technical blogging comes in.

I've been in this game since I was a kid. I've been in this game since I was a kid—I built my first website when I was six years old, believe it or not. Since then, I've worn many hats - developer, team lead, technical consultant, CTO, you name it. Through all the job changes, tech stack switches, and career pivots, my blog has been my constant companion. It's more than just a collection of posts - it's a living document of my journey in tech.

This book is about technical blogging, but it's also about something bigger. It's about creating a lasting record of your growth as a tech professional. It's about sharing what you know, learning from others, and building a reputation that goes beyond any single job or role.

In the chapters ahead, we'll dig into the practical stuff - how to write engaging posts, grow your audience, and use blogging to boost your career. We'll look at the tools that can make blogging easier, and we'll explore how blogging might change as tech evolves.

But more than that, we'll talk about how blogging can become your professional diary - a record of lessons learned, challenges overcome, and skills acquired. It's something I wish someone had told me when I was starting out: your blog posts, your documentation, your shared knowledge - that's what you get to keep. Jobs will come and go, but your blog? That's yours for the long haul.

So whether you're just starting out in tech or you're a seasoned pro, this book is for you. We'll start with the basics in this chapter - what technical blogging is, why it matters, and how to get started.

Remember, every expert was once a beginner. Every influential voice in tech started with a single post. Your experiences, your insights, your "I finally figured it out!" moments - they're all worth sharing.

Ready to start documenting your own tech journey? Let's dive in.

What is Technical Blogging?

Technical blogging is a form of content creation focused on sharing detailed insights, explanations, and perspectives on technology topics. From coding tutorials to software reviews, technical bloggers share their knowledge with a diverse audience of learners, professionals, and tech enthusiasts.

In the evolving digital age, technical blogging has emerged as a significant element of the tech industry, fostering a culture of continuous learning and innovation. It provides a platform where new ideas are introduced, debated, and refined. Unlike traditional blogging, technical blogging often involves:

1. In-depth explanations of complex technical concepts
2. Code snippets and practical examples
3. Tutorials and how-to guides
4. Analysis of new technologies and industry trends
5. Personal experiences with implementing or troubleshooting tech solutions

Technical blogs serve as an invaluable resource for developers at all levels, from beginners looking to understand basic concepts to experienced professionals seeking advanced techniques or solutions to specific problems.

The Challenges and Rewards of Technical Blogging

Technical blogging often presents unique challenges compared to other forms of blogging. It requires a sound understanding of technology, the ability to simplify complex concepts, and a knack for anticipating reader questions. When I first started blogging, I quickly realized that explaining technical concepts clearly and engagingly was no small feat.

One of the primary challenges is staying up-to-date with rapidly evolving technologies. As a blogger, you need to continually learn and adapt to new developments in your field. I later learned that this set of skills is also greatly beneficial for progressing in one's career in tech. This constant learning curve can be demanding, but it's also one of the most rewarding aspects of technical blogging.

Another challenge lies in striking the right balance between depth and accessibility. Your content needs to be technical enough to be useful to experienced developers, yet clear enough to be understood by newcomers to the field. This often requires a careful approach to writing, using analogies, diagrams, and well-commented code examples to illustrate complex ideas.

Despite these challenges, the rewards of technical blogging far outweigh the difficulties:

1. Deepening Your Own Understanding: The process of explaining a concept to others often leads to a deeper understanding of the subject matter yourself. As the saying goes, "To teach is to learn twice."
2. Building a Professional Network: Blogging can connect you with like-minded professionals, potential collaborators, and even future employers.
3. Establishing Authority: Consistently producing high-quality technical content can establish you as an authority in your field.
4. Creating Lasting Resources: Each blog post becomes a potential reference point, not just for readers but for the author as well. The most rewarding posts are those that readers return to time and again, providing a clear, useful guide for a complex problem or concept.
5. Career Advancement: As we'll explore later in this chapter, technical blogging can open up numerous career opportunities.

My first technical blog post was a simple tutorial on finding an online storage solution.

While it seemed basic to me, the positive feedback I received was overwhelming. Readers appreciated the clear, side-by-side comparison, and it taught me the value of sharing even seemingly simple knowledge. This experience encouraged me to continue blogging, tackling increasingly complex topics over time.

Rewards of Technical Blogging

- Deepens your understanding
- Builds professional network
- Establishes authority
- Creates lasting resources

Personal Journey: Learning and Sharing AngularJS

My experience with AngularJS perfectly illustrates the symbiotic relationship between learning and blogging. When I first encountered AngularJS, its structure was unlike anything I'd worked with before. My background in MVC frameworks and backend CMSs didn't immediately apply. It was a labyrinth of new concepts that I was determined to decipher.

As I delved into AngularJS, I realized the importance of documenting my journey. Not just for my own reference, but as a beacon for others sailing in the same seas. My blog became a living document of this learning journey, providing a route map for others to follow or diverge from as they explored AngularJS.

One of the most significant "lightbulb moments" was discovering the utility of adding configuration to an AngularJS app. Realizing that a centralized location for injecting variables could vastly improve code manageability was a game-changer. I immediately wrote a blog post about this insight, eager to share this nugget of wisdom that could simplify others' AngularJS journeys. To this day it is one of my most popular posts.

Another crucial discovery was understanding the proper way of filtering with AngularJS—utilizing filter:filterService.getFilter() for selective item filtration. These illuminating discoveries, while seemingly minor, were significant in shaping my understanding of AngularJS and, in turn, assisting others.

The process of learning and blogging about AngularJS taught me several valuable lessons:

1. Breaking Down Complex Concepts: AngularJS introduced many new paradigms. By explaining these in my blog posts, I learned to break down complex ideas into more digestible parts.
2. The Power of Examples: I found that including practical, real-world examples in my posts greatly enhanced understanding, both for my readers and myself.
3. The Importance of Context: Explaining why certain AngularJS features were designed in specific ways helped readers (and me) understand the bigger picture of the framework's architecture.
4. Community Engagement: The comments and questions I received on my AngularJS posts often led to deeper explorations and sometimes even corrections to my understanding.

This journey with AngularJS was transformative, not just in terms of learning a new technology, but in shaping my approach to technical blogging. It taught me the value of sharing the learning process, not just the end results.

The Impact of Technical Blogging on the Tech Community

The impact of technical blogging on the tech community cannot be overstated. It has become, in essence, how software engineers teach one another. It serves as a repository of shared knowledge, hard-won insights, and time-saving solutions. This knowledge exchange fosters an environment of accelerated learning and camaraderie.

Technical blogs contribute to the community in several key ways:

1. Knowledge Democratization: Blogs make specialized knowledge accessible to anyone with an internet connection, democratizing learning in the tech field.
2. Real-World Problem Solving: Many technical blogs document solutions to real-world problems, saving other developers time and effort.
3. Trend Analysis and Forecasting: Bloggers often discuss emerging technologies and industry trends, helping the community stay ahead of the curve.
4. Code Sharing: Through code snippets and project examples, bloggers share practical implementations that others can learn from or build upon.
5. Fostering Discussion: Comment sections and social media sharing of blog posts create spaces for further discussion and idea exchange.

Sites like Y Combinator's HackerNews exemplify this impact. They teem with rich, in-depth stories of engineers wrestling with complicated issues, sharing their journeys, their solutions, and their lessons learned. As we contribute to and draw from this shared pool of knowledge, we foster a culture of collaborative learning and innovation.

My personal blog, Kidsil.net, evolved from a personal reference into an archive of knowledge for others. The Mean.js series I wrote is a prime example. These articles not only resonated with the tech community but also caught the attention of the original Mean.js developers, leading to further collaboration on content creation and core development work.

This experience highlighted another crucial aspect of technical blogging: the potential for collaboration and networking. By sharing our knowledge, we open doors to connect with others in the field, including the creators and maintainers of the technologies we write about.

Moreover, technical blogging plays a vital role in the open-source community. Many bloggers document their experiences with open-source tools, provide tutorials, and even contribute improvements or bug fixes based on their explorations. This symbiotic relationship between blogging and open-source development accelerates innovation and improves the quality of open-source software.

In essence, technical blogging creates a virtuous cycle of learning, sharing, and improving that benefits the entire tech ecosystem.

Case Study: Google Cloud Platform Migration

In 2014, I embarked on a bold journey to migrate all my websites from an old shared hosting platform to Google Cloud Platform (GCP). This adventure, which started with winning GCP credits in a local Google competition, became a significant learning experience and a rich source of content for my blog.

The migration process was far from straightforward and presented numerous challenges:

1. Email Server Setup: In my previous shared hosting environment, email servers were a built-in feature. However, on GCP, I discovered that Google Compute Engine blocked all outgoing traffic to port 25, the standard port for email transmission. This unexpected hurdle led me to explore and document the process of configuring email forwarding using a third-party service.
2. Learning Cloud Architecture: Moving from shared hosting to a cloud platform required a paradigm shift in how I thought about web hosting. I had to learn about virtual machines, network configurations, and cloud-specific security measures.
3. Performance Optimization: While the cloud offered more power and flexibility, it also required careful optimization to ensure cost-effective performance.

However, the real shock came when I woke up one morning to find my servers had been compromised, merely 10 hours after the migration. This incident became the basis for one of my most impactful blog posts: "How I got hacked in 10 hours on Google Cloud Platform."

This post wasn't just a recounting of my ordeal; it was a valuable learning experience for me and my readers. It demonstrated how swiftly vulnerabilities could be exploited in a cloud environment and emphasized the importance of robust security measures. The post covered several key points:

1. The importance of immediate security measures when setting up a new cloud instance.
2. Common vulnerabilities that attackers look for in cloud environments.
3. Steps to take after a security breach.

4. Lessons learned about ongoing security maintenance in the cloud.

The post generated significant engagement, sparking discussions about cloud security and leading to improvements in my own security practices. It also highlighted the value of sharing not just successes, but also failures and challenges in technical blogging.

This experience led to several important realizations:

1. The Need for Continuous Learning: The rapidly evolving nature of cloud technologies means that staying updated is crucial.
2. The Value of Community Knowledge: Many readers shared additional security tips in the comments, enriching the post with their own experiences.
3. The Importance of Documentation: Thoroughly documenting the migration process and subsequent issues helped me create a valuable resource for others attempting similar migrations.
4. Turning Setbacks into Opportunities: What started as a discouraging security breach became an opportunity to learn, share knowledge, and engage with the tech community.

In response to this incident, I made a swift decision to transition from WordPress to static site generators like Jekyll and Hugo. This decision was driven by a desire for increased security and control over my websites. Static websites offer enhanced security as they do not rely on databases and are less vulnerable to attacks.

This migration to static site generators became another rich source of blog content. I documented the process, the challenges faced, and the benefits realized. These posts not only helped others considering similar transitions but also deepened my understanding of web technologies and security practices.

From Blogging to Career Advancement

What started as a way to document my learning and experiences soon became a powerful career advancement tool. My blog served as more than just an avenue for sharing experiences; it became an irrefutable testament to my skills and knowledge.

Here are some ways in which blogging directly impacted my career:

1. Showcasing Expertise: My series of posts on AngularJS demonstrated not just my technical knowledge, but also my ability to explain complex concepts clearly. This caught the attention of potential employers and clients.
2. Opening New Opportunities: The visibility gained from my blog led to unexpected opportunities. For instance, a national airline company reached out to me for a consulting role based on my AngularJS posts.
3. Building a Personal Brand: Consistent blogging helped me establish a personal brand in the tech community. This brand became a valuable asset in job negotiations and client acquisitions.
4. Continuous Learning: The discipline of regular blogging kept me on a path of continuous learning, which in turn made me a more valuable professional.
5. Networking: My blog became a conversation starter at tech meetups and conferences, helping me build a robust professional network.

One particularly impactful experience was when my posts about bridging the knowledge gap between tech and non-tech departments in companies caught the attention of recruiters. This led to fruitful relationships with recruitment professionals, further expanding my network within the industry.

Another interesting venture that stemmed from my blogging was the launch of an event aggregation app named "Berlin on Feier". This app collected events from around Berlin and provided users with a comprehensive database of local events. While the app itself faced challenges in partnership discussions, the underlying aggregation engine became an open-source project that won me $20K in Google Cloud Platform credits.

This experience reinforced a crucial lesson: in the world of technical blogging, sharing both successes and failures can lead to unexpected opportunities. The tech community values authenticity and learning from real-world experiences, both positive and negative.

Tools and Techniques: Enhancing the Blogging Process

Over time, I've developed a set of tools and techniques that have significantly enhanced my blogging process. These tools not only improve efficiency but also help maintain the quality and consistency of my content.

Emacs: A Distraction-Free Writing Environment

Central to my blogging workflow is Emacs, a powerful text editor that provides a distraction-free writing environment. By avoiding browser-based tools, I can create a dedicated space for focused writing, free from the temptations of social media or email notifications.

Key benefits of using Emacs for blogging include:

1. Customizability: Emacs allows for extensive customization, enabling me to tailor the editor to my specific needs.

2. Keyboard-centric workflow: With Emacs, I can perform most tasks without taking my hands off the keyboard, increasing efficiency.
3. Version control integration: Easy integration with Git allows for efficient management of blog post drafts and revisions.
4. Cross-platform consistency: Emacs provides a consistent environment across different operating systems, which is crucial for my workflow.

Orgmode: The Swiss Army Knife of Content Organization

Orgmode, an Emacs package, has revolutionized how I organize my thoughts and manage my content. It's more than just a tool; it's an ecosystem that aids in organizing thoughts, creating to-do lists, and even tracking time.

Some key features of Orgmode that I find invaluable for blogging include:

1. Hierarchical structure: Easily organize ideas and sections of a blog post.
2. TODO lists: Manage tasks related to blog post creation, from research to publishing.
3. Code block execution: Test code snippets directly within the document.
4. Export functionality: Easily convert Orgmode documents to various formats, including HTML for blog posts.

Streamlining the Workflow

The combination of Emacs and Orgmode allows for a streamlined blogging workflow:

1. Idea Capture: Quickly jot down blog post ideas in an Orgmode file.
2. Outlining: Use Orgmode's hierarchical structure to create a detailed outline.
3. Writing: Leverage Emacs' distraction-free environment for focused writing.
4. Code Integration: Use Orgmode's code blocks to include and test code snippets.
5. Editing: Utilize Emacs' powerful editing features for efficient revisions.
6. Publishing: Export the finished post to the appropriate format for the blog platform.

Overcoming Challenges in Tool Adoption

It's important to note that the journey to optimizing these tools was not without challenges. For instance, transitioning from Spacemacs (a pre-configured distribution of Emacs) to a leaner Emacs setup required learning new shortcuts and adapting my workflow.

The process involved:

1. Identifying essential features: Determining which Spacemacs features were crucial for my workflow.
2. Minimal configuration: Building a lean Emacs configuration that included only necessary packages.

3. Learning curve: Investing time to learn Emacs' native shortcuts and commands.
4. Continuous refinement: Regularly tweaking the setup based on changing needs and discoveries.

While this transition period required effort and patience, the resulting increase in efficiency has been well worth it. My current setup is lean, fast, and tailored specifically to my blogging needs.

The Power of Static Site Generators

In addition to Emacs and Orgmode, I've found great value in using static site generators for my blog. After my experience with security issues on WordPress, I transitioned to Jekyll and later to Hugo.

Benefits of static site generators for blogging include:

1. Improved security: With no database or server-side scripts, static sites are less vulnerable to common web attacks.
2. Speed: Static pages load faster, improving user experience and SEO.
3. Cost and Scale: The cost of running a static website with tens of thousands of readers is roughly $0.02 a month, including images, diagrams, and other media.
4. Version control: Easy integration with Git for managing content and collaboration.
5. Markdown support: Write content in Markdown, which is easier to manage and less prone to formatting issues.

The transition to static site generators was a learning experience in itself, providing material for several blog posts and deepening my understanding of web technologies.

Conclusion

Technical blogging is more than just a way to share knowledge; it's a journey of continuous learning, a tool for career advancement, and a means of contributing to the tech community. Through my own experiences—from deciphering AngularJS to navigating cloud migrations—I've found that every challenge presents an opportunity to learn and share.

The tools and techniques we use in our blogging process can significantly impact our efficiency and the quality of our output. While there might be a learning curve associated with tools like Emacs and Orgmode, the long-term benefits in terms of productivity and content quality are substantial.

As we move forward in this book, we'll delve deeper into the specifics of creating compelling technical content, growing your blog, and leveraging your online presence for career opportunities. We'll explore how to choose topics that resonate with your audience, how to structure your posts for maximum impact, and how to promote your content effectively.

Whether you're just starting your blogging journey or looking to enhance your existing blog, the chapters ahead will provide you with practical insights and strategies to make your voice heard in the vast landscape of technology.

In the next chapter, we'll explore the nuts and bolts of setting up your technical blog, from choosing a platform to creating your first post. We'll also discuss how to find your unique voice and niche in the crowded world of tech blogging. So, let's embark on this exciting journey of technical blogging together!

CHAPTER 2

Embracing the Tools of the Trade

In the world of technical blogging, the tools you choose can significantly impact your productivity, efficiency, and the quality of your content. This chapter delves into the various tools and philosophies that have shaped my approach to technical writing and software development. From the organizational power of Orgmode to the transformative influence of open-source software, we'll explore how the right tools can not only enhance your blogging process but also contribute to your overall growth as a technology professional.

My journey with these tools began early in my career and has continually evolved. Each tool and philosophy I've adopted has played a crucial role in shaping my work methods and, by extension, the content I produce. As we explore these tools and approaches, I encourage you to consider how they might fit into your own workflow and potentially transform your technical blogging journey.

Orgmode: A Powerhouse for Organization and Productivity

At the heart of my technical blogging workflow lies Orgmode, an Emacs package that has revolutionized how I organize my thoughts, manage tasks, and structure my work. Orgmode is more than just a note-taking tool; it's a comprehensive system for managing projects, writing documents, and organizing your life.

Orgmode has deeply influenced my work as well, helping me manage vast amounts of information across numerous clients, prioritize TODOs and deadlines, and keep tabs on my agenda. Being a minimal text-based tool, it has helped me stay mobile at all times by allowing me to quickly open notes on my phone when I'm not on my laptop, ensuring I don't miss any note-taking opportunities.

Overview of Orgmode and its Features

Orgmode's power lies in its flexibility and extensibility. At its core, it's a system for maintaining plain text files with a special syntax that allows for complex structuring of information. Some of its key features include:

1. Hierarchical structure: Easily organize ideas and sections using a simple, intuitive outlining system.
2. TODO lists: Create and manage tasks directly within your documents.
3. Tags: Categorize and filter information quickly.
4. Priorities: Add priorities to any task for advanced sorting and filtering.
5. Tables: Create and manipulate tables with spreadsheet-like functionality.

6. Code blocks: Include and execute code snippets in various programming languages.

These features combine to create a powerful environment for both writing and task management, making it an ideal tool for technical bloggers who often juggle multiple projects and ideas.

Task Management with DEADLINE and SCHEDULED

Two of Orgmode's most powerful features for task management are the DEADLINE and SCHEDULED keywords. According to Orgmode's documentation, these are used in combination with timestamps to facilitate planning:

- DEADLINE: This signifies the date by which a task should ideally be finished. From a set number of days before this deadline, Orgmode starts issuing warnings about the task's impending due date in the agenda, continuing until the task is marked as done.
- SCHEDULED: This refers to the date on which one plans to start working on a task. The task appears in the agenda on the scheduled date, with reminders appearing if the date has passed and the task is yet to be completed.

Here's an example of how these might look in an Orgmode file:

```
* TODO Write blog post on Orgmode
SCHEDULED: <2023-07-20 Thu> DEADLINE: <2023-07-25 Tue>
```

This simple syntax allows for powerful task tracking and time management.

Repeated Tasks and Their Impact on Workflow

Another feature of Orgmode that significantly boosted my productivity is the ability to set up repeated tasks. This feature is particularly useful for managing recurring responsibilities, such as weekly blog posts, monthly newsletter drafts, or regular code reviews.

Here's an example of a repeated task in Orgmode:

```
* TODO Review and update blog content
  SCHEDULED: <2023-07-01 Sat +1m>
```

This sets up a task that repeats monthly (+1m). Orgmode will automatically reschedule this task for the next month once it's marked as done.

Personal Experience: How Orgmode Transformed My Work Routine

Employing Orgmode's task management features like DEADLINE, SCHEDULED, and repeated tasks fundamentally transformed my work routine. Each task was now accompanied by a clear commencement plan (SCHEDULED) and a hard end-point (DEADLINE). This structure empowered me to better control my workflow and provided a clear overview of my projects.

The use of repeated tasks helped to keep recurring duties in check, thus minimizing the chances of overlooking or neglecting them. For instance, I set up recurring tasks for:

1. Weekly content brainstorming sessions
2. Monthly blog performance reviews

3. Quarterly technology trend research

This system ensured that these important but easily forgettable tasks were always on my radar.

Moreover, the practice of subdividing tasks into manageable pieces played a significant role in enhancing my efficiency. Each subtask, having its own TODO and allocated times, could be approached and completed as an individual entity. This eliminated the daunting prospect of a large task and instead presented a series of smaller, more manageable tasks. The sense of progress from ticking off these 'mini-tasks' also provided a motivational boost.

For example, when working on a complex technical blog post, I might break it down like this:

```
* TODO Write blog post on Advanced Docker Techniques
** TODO Research latest Docker features
SCHEDULED: <2023-07-15 Sat>
** TODO Outline main points of the article
SCHEDULED: <2023-07-16 Sun>
** TODO Write first draft
SCHEDULED: <2023-07-18 Tue>
** TODO Create code examples
SCHEDULED: <2023-07-20 Thu>
** TODO Review and edit
SCHEDULED: <2023-07-22 Sat>
** TODO Publish post
DEADLINE: <2023-07-25 Tue>
```

This structure allowed me to focus on one aspect at a time, making the overall task less overwhelming and more manageable.

The Philosophy of Minimalism in Tools

While Orgmode's features are extensive, my approach to using it, and indeed all my tools, is guided by a philosophy of minimalism. This principle, which is a product of years of using Linux from Red Hat 5 to Ubuntu, became a defining characteristic of my approach towards tools and software.

The Influence of Linux on Tool Selection

My journey with Linux has had a profound impact on my work approach. Linux, in essence, champions the use of smart, light tools - a philosophy I have embraced wholeheartedly. This Operating System embodies the idea that tools should be efficient, customizable, and focused on doing one thing well.

This very philosophy of having small, composable tools that can be chained together to perform complex tasks has influenced how I approach problem-solving in my work. Instead of reaching for large, monolithic applications, I often find myself creating workflows that combine several smaller, more focused tools.

Prioritizing Functionality over Aesthetics

In my professional work, visual aesthetics take a back seat to functionality and efficiency. This doesn't mean that I don't appreciate good design, but rather that I prioritize tools that allow me to get my work done effectively and efficiently.

For example, when choosing between a visually appealing but resource-heavy IDE and a lighter, more customizable text editor like Emacs, I opt for the latter. The key is to leverage my hardware's capabilities to their fullest extent for running servers, Docker containers, and development environments, rather than for superficial visual effects.

The Lean Approach to Orgmode and Other Tools

This approach extends to my usage of Orgmode, wherein I have trimmed it down to a lean tool, focusing on functionality over visual appeal. Instead of using all of Orgmode's features, I've identified the core functionalities that serve my workflow best and stick to those.

For instance, while Orgmode offers a robust agenda view with many customization options, I've streamlined my setup to show only the most critical information:

```
(setq org-agenda-custom-commands
'(("n" "Agenda and all TODOs"
((agenda "" nil)
(alltodo "" nil))
nil)))
```

This simple configuration gives me a clear overview of my scheduled tasks and todos without overwhelming me with excessive information.

Similarly, I've applied this lean approach to other tools in my workflow:

1. Emacs configuration: I maintain a minimal .emacs file, adding only the features I regularly use.
2. Shell scripts: I write focused, single-purpose scripts that can be combined for more complex operations.
3. Git workflow: I use a straightforward branching strategy, avoiding overly complex workflows that can hinder productivity.

4. Music: I use a mixture of Cmus, a CLI-based music player, and Zsh aliases to listen and stream music from the command line."

The mindset of striving for efficiency and simplicity served as a core philosophy, impacting not just my interaction with Emacs and Orgmode, but also my overall approach to learning and using new tools.

The Power of Open Source

One of the most critical insights from my professional journey has been the undeniable advantage that open-source solutions often hold over their proprietary counterparts. This belief is rooted in my years of Linux use, which began in 1997 when I was just 8 years old, and my deep dive into the open-source ecosystem.

Advantages of Open-Source Solutions

Open-source software allows for a transparency that you wouldn't get in proprietary software. With open-source, you can:

1. Look under the hood: Examine the source code to understand how the software works.
2. Identify potential issues: Spot and report bugs or security vulnerabilities.
3. Contribute improvements: Submit patches or new features to enhance the software.
4. Customize to your needs: Modify the software to better suit your specific requirements.

This fosters an environment of continuous learning and improvement - a perfect match for the dynamic, ever-evolving landscape of technology.

Moreover, open-source solutions often breed innovation due to their collaborative nature. Developers from around the world can contribute, each bringing their unique perspective and expertise. This results in software that's not only robust and versatile but also tailored to meet a diverse range of needs.

Personal Journey with Open-Source Technologies

My journey with open-source technologies began very early in my career. As a teenager, I was drawn to Linux, fascinated by the idea of an operating system that I could explore, modify, and understand at a fundamental level. This early exposure to open-source principles shaped my approach to software development and problem-solving.

Some key milestones in my open-source journey include:

1. Installing my first Linux distribution (Red Hat Linux 5, released 1997) and learning to navigate the command line.
2. Contributing libraries and extensions to renowned open source projects, several PHP-based Content Management Systems.
3. Publishing patches to a small open-source project, fixing a bug in a Python library.
4. Developing and releasing my own open-source tools, including a data aggregation engine that won recognition in a Google-sponsored competition.

Each of these experiences not only enhanced my technical skills but also deepened my appreciation for the open-source ethos of collaboration and knowledge sharing.

Impact on Career Development and Technical Skills

This belief in the power of open source has played a fundamental role in guiding my technical decisions and shaping my professional trajectory. From choosing Linux over other operating systems to building robust data aggregation tools using Python-based libraries, my journey has been enriched and enabled by the open-source ecosystem.

The impact on my career development has been significant:

1. Skill Acquisition: Working with open-source technologies exposed me to a wide range of coding styles, design patterns, and best practices. This accelerated my learning and broadened my skill set.
2. Problem-Solving Abilities: Debugging open-source software and contributing patches honed my problem-solving skills, teaching me to approach issues methodically and creatively.
3. Community Engagement: Participating in open-source communities improved my communication skills and taught me how to collaborate effectively with developers from diverse backgrounds.
4. Career Opportunities: My experience with open-source technologies opened doors to job opportunities and consulting gigs that might otherwise have been inaccessible.

For instance, using open-source technologies like PHP and Python equipped me with an invaluable wealth of DevOps and system administration knowledge early on. This knowledge, along with the projects I built using these open-source technologies, bolstered my resume and helped me sail smoothly through interviews.

Practical Applications and Contributions

My interactions with open-source haven't been limited to just usage and learning. I've actively contributed to the open-source community in various ways, each experience deepening my understanding and honing my skills.

Examples of Open-Source Contributions

1. Django Timestamp Issue: When Django, a high-level Python web framework, faced an issue with timestamp calculations, I stepped in to help resolve it. This experience not only improved my understanding of Django's internals but also taught me about the intricacies of working with timestamps in web applications.
2. WordPress Plugins: My contributions to WordPress were more extensive. I developed several plugins, with one specifically designed to streamline the process of packaging and auto-updating plugins in groups. This project required a deep dive into WordPress's plugin architecture and update mechanisms, significantly enhancing my PHP skills and understanding of content management systems.
3. Firefox Extension: I have written a Firefox extension to fully remove notifications from muted tabs. While personally it has helped me silence Slack and WhatsApp windows, I found it meaningful to share it with others who may find it useful.
4. Drupal Modules: I also contributed to the Drupal ecosystem by developing custom modules. This experience broadened my understanding of different CMS architectures and reinforced my PHP skills in a different context.
5. Data Aggregation Library: I have released code for a Python-based data aggregation library I developed. This project involved consolidating various data sources into a unified format, coincidentally it also won me $20K in Google Cloud Credits.

These contributions, while varying in scale, all provided valuable learning experiences and allowed me to give back to the communities that had supported my growth as a developer.

Learning Opportunities in the Open-Source Community

Engaging with open-source projects presents aspiring developers with certain advantages. From the early stages of their learning journey, they are exposed to high-level coding standards demanded by most open-source repositories. This experience often mirrors the professional work environment, providing valuable insights that far outweigh conventional learning methods.

Some key learning opportunities include:

1. Code Review Process: Submitting pull requests and going through code reviews teaches you how to write clean, maintainable code and how to accept and incorporate feedback.
2. Documentation: Contributing to or improving project documentation hones your technical writing skills, crucial for any developer.
3. Issue Tracking: Engaging with issue trackers teaches you how to report bugs effectively and how to manage and prioritize tasks in a development environment.
4. Community Interaction: Participating in discussions, helping other users, and collaborating with maintainers improves your communication skills and teaches you how to work in a distributed team.

The Role of Open Source in Staying Current with Technology Trends

By being an active part of the open-source community, developers can stay informed about the latest technology trends and advancements. This is a crucial aspect of career growth and development in the ever-evolving field of technology.

Open source projects often serve as incubators for new technologies and methodologies. By engaging with these projects, you can:

1. Get early exposure to emerging technologies: Many cutting-edge tools and frameworks start as open-source projects before gaining widespread adoption.
2. Understand industry best practices: Open-source projects often implement and showcase current best practices in software development.
3. Learn from expert developers: By reading code written by experienced developers and participating in discussions, you can learn advanced techniques and approaches.
4. Stay informed about technology shifts: The open-source community is often quick to adopt and implement new technological paradigms, giving you a window into where the industry is heading.

For instance, my early involvement with projects using containerization technologies like Docker gave me a head start when these tools became industry standards. Similarly, engaging with machine learning libraries in their early stages prepared me for the AI and data science boom that followed.

Navigating the Proprietary-Open Source Divide

While open-source software has been instrumental in my career, it's important to acknowledge that proprietary software also plays a significant role in the tech industry. Navigating this divide requires careful consideration and often involves weighing the benefits and drawbacks of each approach.

Comparison with Proprietary Software (Silverlight Example)

Reflecting on my career, I recall a particularly enlightening incident involving a friend who was fully invested in Microsoft's Silverlight and C#. This situation highlighted some of the key differences between proprietary and open-source approaches.

I asked my friend two critical questions:

1. Was he capable of running his code on non-Windows servers?
2. Was he concerned about the future trajectory of Silverlight?

These questions touched on two fundamental issues with proprietary software:

1. Platform Dependency: Proprietary solutions often tie you to a specific platform or ecosystem, limiting flexibility and potentially increasing costs.
2. Uncertain Future: The development and support of proprietary software are at the discretion of a single company. If the company decides to discontinue or significantly alter the product, developers relying on it can face significant challenges.

In this case, the very core of my friend's project was in the hands of the Silverlight team. This reliance on a single entity for the future of his work made me apprehensive. Silverlight's inactivity since 2012 and its complete discontinuation in 2019 highlighted these concerns even more. It showed the real risk of investing heavily in proprietary technology that might not have a guaranteed future.

This story illustrates a major issue with proprietary software. By its nature, it is limiting, putting the users at the mercy of a single entity, which determines its direction and support. While proprietary software can offer robust, well-supported solutions, it also introduces risks and limitations that developers should carefully consider.

Long-term Benefits of Open-Source Adoption

In contrast, open-source software offers several long-term benefits:

1. Longevity: Open-source projects often have longer lifespans. Tools like Linux, Emacs, Vim, and Python have not only survived but thrived over many years, adapting to changing technological landscapes and user requirements.
2. Community Support: Even if the original creators move on, a strong community can continue to maintain and evolve the software.
3. Transparency: The ability to inspect and modify the source code provides a level of control and understanding that's not possible with proprietary solutions.
4. Flexibility: Open-source software can often be customized and adapted to specific needs more easily than proprietary alternatives.
5. Cost-Effectiveness: While open-source doesn't always mean free, it often provides a more cost-effective solution, especially for startups and individual developers.

Building a Career Foundation with Open-Source Technologies

My experience has shown that using open-source technologies can provide a solid foundation for building a successful career in technology. Here's how:

1. Early Practical Experience: One of the key benefits of open-source software is the ability to get your hands dirty and dive into project development early on, even as a teenager. This was particularly true for me. The availability and accessibility of open-source projects allowed me to acquire practical experience and build a portfolio long before stepping foot into an office environment.
2. Diverse Skill Set: Working with open-source technologies often requires you to understand various aspects of software development, from coding to deployment to maintenance. This broad exposure can make you a more versatile and valuable professional.
3. Community Networking: Engaging with open-source communities can help you build a professional network, potentially leading to job opportunities or collaborations.
4. Demonstrated Initiative: Contributing to open-source projects shows potential employers that you're passionate about technology and capable of self-directed learning and work.
5. Relevant Skills: Many companies use open-source technologies in their stack. Experience with these tools can make you an attractive candidate.

In my case, the knowledge and projects I built using open-source technologies significantly bolstered my resume. During job interviews, I could point to concrete contributions I had made to real-world projects, which set me apart from other candidates.

Conclusion

As we conclude this chapter on embracing the tools of the trade, it's clear that the choices we make regarding our tools and technologies can have a profound impact on our productivity, learning, and career trajectory.

Orgmode, with its powerful organizational capabilities, demonstrates how the right tool can transform your workflow and boost productivity. The philosophy of minimalism, influenced by my experiences with Linux, shows the value of prioritizing functionality and efficiency over unnecessary complexity.

Perhaps most significantly, the open-source ecosystem has proven to be an invaluable resource for learning, growth, and career advancement. From providing early hands-on experience to offering opportunities for meaningful contributions, open-source technologies have shaped my journey in countless ways.

As you continue your own journey in technical blogging and software development, I encourage you to:

1. Explore and experiment with different tools to find what works best for your workflow.
2. Embrace minimalism and efficiency in your choice and use of tools.
3. Engage with the open-source community - use open-source tools, contribute to projects, and share your knowledge.
4. Consider the long-term implications of the technologies you choose to invest your time in.

Keep in mind, the tools we use are more than just means to an end - they shape our thinking, influence our approach to problem-solving, and can open doors to new opportunities. Choose wisely, stay curious, and never stop learning.

In the next chapter, we'll dive into the art of crafting compelling technical content, exploring techniques to make your blog posts informative, engaging, and impactful. We'll draw on the organizational skills developed through tools like Orgmode and the collaborative spirit of open-source to create content that resonates with your audience and establishes you as an expert in your field.

CHAPTER 3

Crafting Compelling Technical Content

In the ever-evolving landscape of technology, personal experience often serves as the most valuable teacher. This chapter delves into my journey as a technical blogger, highlighting the pivotal moments, challenges, and insights that have shaped my career. From exploring niche technologies to overcoming the hurdles of emerging platforms, this narrative aims to provide aspiring bloggers and tech enthusiasts with practical wisdom and inspiration.

My path in technical blogging has been one of continuous learning, experimentation, and adaptation. It's a testament to the power of curiosity and the willingness to venture into uncharted territories. Through this chapter, I hope to illustrate how embracing new technologies, understanding your audience, and maintaining a commitment to quality can not only enhance your blog but also open doors to exciting professional opportunities.

Leveraging and Embracing Cutting-Edge Technologies

The Power of Curiosity

My journey into the realm of cutting-edge technologies began out of sheer curiosity and a desire to explore beyond the conventional. I found myself delving into emerging areas of software development that many might shy away from due to their complexity. This unique approach to learning technology not only satiated my intellectual curiosity but also opened up a world of opportunities for me.

AngularJS: Conquering the Steep Learning Curve

One of the first cutting-edge technologies I tackled was AngularJS. At the time, AngularJS was notorious for its steep learning curve, which deterred many developers from adopting it. Initially, I used AngularJS only for personal projects, grappling with its complex features and exploring its capabilities. The learning process was challenging, often frustrating, but I persevered where others had given up.

I distinctly remember the 'eureka' moment when I finally understood the power of AngularJS's dependency injection system. Understanding how to use the $injector service to manually bootstrap Angular applications and inject dependencies gave me a deeper appreciation for the framework's flexibility and testability. This knowledge proved crucial in developing more modular and maintainable applications.

As I began to master these intricacies, I realized the potential value of sharing my hard-won insights with others. I started publishing detailed blog posts about the library, showcasing unique solutions to common problems and demonstrating my growing proficiency. To my surprise, these posts began to gain significant traction. I noticed that my visibility in the tech community started to rise rapidly. People began recognizing me as an expert in AngularJS, one of the few who had conquered its steep learning curve.

This recognition translated into tangible benefits - it greatly helped in securing freelance contracts. Recruiters, desperate to find AngularJS talent in a market where demand far outstripped supply, began reaching out to me directly.

The key takeaway from this experience was the power of tackling challenging, cutting-edge technologies and consistently sharing that knowledge. By immersing myself in a difficult but highly sought-after technology and then articulating my understanding through blog posts, I was able to establish myself as a go-to resource in an area where expertise was scarce and valuable.

Mean.js: Filling the Documentation Gap

Another technology that caught my attention was Mean.js. I noticed that while this framework was quite powerful, it lacked comprehensive documentation. This gap presented an opportunity - not just to learn the technology myself, but to create value for others in the process.

I embarked on creating guides and tutorials to fill this documentation gap. These articles proved immensely popular, further solidifying my standing in the tech community as a knowledgeable authority in the field. This experience taught me an important lesson: sometimes, the most valuable contribution you can make is not in creating new technologies, but in making existing ones more accessible and understandable.

TypeScript: Leveraging Strong Typing in Backend Development

My transition to TypeScript for backend development was catalyzed by a renewed appreciation for strong typing, rekindled during my work with Go. The parallel concepts of interfaces, generics, and type inference in Go provided a cognitive bridge, allowing me to rapidly adapt to TypeScript's simpler type system. This synergy between languages exemplified how diverse programming experiences can accelerate learning and adaptation in the ever-evolving tech landscape.

TypeScript's advanced features like union types, intersection types, and mapped types enabled me to create more robust, self-documenting code. This proficiency opened doors to high-value projects, particularly in building scalable, type-safe APIs and microservices using frameworks like NestJS. The ability to ensure type safety across the entire application stack positioned me as a sought-after lead developer, capable of delivering end-to-end solutions with enhanced reliability and maintainability.

The key insight from this experience was the multiplicative value of transferable knowledge across technologies. By leveraging my background in Go to quickly master TypeScript, I not only expanded my technical repertoire but also refined my approach to software design, emphasizing clarity and correctness through type systems. This adaptability proved crucial in freelance development, enabling me to align swiftly with market demands and offer clients cutting-edge, quality-driven solutions.

The Freelancing Edge

The cornerstone of a successful freelancing career lies in mastering high-demand, complex technologies. Clients seek experts who can navigate intricate technical landscapes and are willing to invest heavily in such expertise. By establishing yourself as an authority in cutting-edge areas, you differentiate yourself in a saturated market, attracting premium projects and commanding higher rates.

This strategy of continuous learning and knowledge sharing keeps you at the cutting edge of technological innovation. It transforms you from a commodity developer into a valued technical partner, ensuring your skills remain not just relevant, but coveted. In the rapidly evolving tech industry, this approach provides a resilient foundation for long-term career stability and growth, allowing you to adapt swiftly to emerging trends and consistently deliver high-impact solutions to clients.

The Meteor.js Experience

My experience with Meteor.js in 2015 provides a solid example of leveraging the capabilities of emerging technologies for real-world projects. At the time, Meteor.js was still a relatively young and unknown framework. However, it presented an exciting opportunity to explore advanced concepts like async/await even before they were supported by vanilla Node.js.

One of the most intriguing aspects of Meteor.js was its concept of "magic binding," a paradigm similar to what we now see in React.js. This feature allowed for real-time, reactive user interfaces with minimal boilerplate code. Leveraging this capability, I was able to develop an innovative MVP (Minimum Viable Product) for a new venture.

The process of learning and implementing Meteor.js taught me several valuable lessons:

1. Early Adoption Advantages: By embracing a new technology early, I was able to offer unique solutions that weren't widely available in the market.
2. Transferable Concepts: Even though Meteor.js itself didn't become mainstream, the concepts I learned (like reactive programming) were applicable to other modern frameworks.
3. Problem-Solving Skills: Working with a less-documented technology honed my problem-solving abilities, as I often had to figure things out without extensive resources.
4. Community Engagement: Being an early adopter allowed me to engage more deeply with the framework's community, contributing to discussions and sometimes even to the framework itself.

This experience underscored the importance of being at the cutting edge of technology trends. Demonstrating the ability to adapt to new libraries and frameworks sets the stage for outstanding opportunities in the freelancing world. Clients often seek developers who can bring fresh, innovative solutions to their projects.

Moreover, embracing new technologies and keeping up with evolving software engineering trends can give a freelance developer a competitive edge. It positions you as a forward-thinking professional who's not afraid to explore and implement cutting-edge solutions.

The Power of Cross-Pollination

Throughout my journey with various technologies, I've discovered the immense value of cross-pollination between different frameworks and languages. Each new technology I've learned has provided unique insights that have enhanced my understanding and application of others. For instance, the reactive programming concepts I mastered in Meteor.js later proved invaluable when working with React and other modern frontend frameworks. This cross-pollination of ideas not only broadens your skill set but also deepens your overall understanding of software architecture and design patterns. It enables you to approach problems from multiple angles and often leads to more innovative solutions, a quality highly prized by clients in the freelance world.

Exploring Emerging Technologies: The Case of Rust

As I continue to explore new technologies, I find myself intrigued by the potential of Rust. While it's still speculative, some developers believe it could become a significant player in building compact, intelligent, and efficient command-line utilities, potentially succeeding languages like Golang in certain areas.

Diving into Rust presents several exciting prospects:

1. Performance: Rust's focus on performance and safety makes it an excellent choice for systems programming and other performance-critical applications.
2. Memory Safety: Rust's unique ownership model promises to eliminate many common programming errors at compile-time, potentially leading to more robust software.
3. Cross-Platform Development: Rust's ability to compile to various targets makes it versatile for developing cross-platform applications.
4. Growing Ecosystem: As Rust gains popularity, its ecosystem of libraries and tools is expanding, opening up new possibilities for development.

5. Career Opportunities: As more companies adopt Rust, expertise in this language could open up new freelance and career opportunities.

While it's too early to definitively claim Rust as the future, exploring it represents the kind of forward-thinking approach that can keep a developer ahead of the curve. It's a reminder that in the tech industry, being open to emerging technologies and continuously learning isn't just beneficial—it's essential for staying relevant and competitive.

Overcoming Challenges with Emerging Technologies

While embracing new technologies can be exciting and rewarding, it often comes with its own set of challenges. One of the most memorable projects I undertook involved developing an authentication system using only serverless technology. This experience exemplifies the hurdles one might face when working with emerging technologies, as well as the valuable lessons and growth opportunities they present.

The Serverless Authentication Challenge

At the time of this project, Serverless was a relatively young technology, and its documentation was limited, particularly for complex use cases. The task at hand was to implement OAuth without a traditional server to handle redirects and manage token expiry. This presented a significant challenge, as most existing OAuth implementations relied heavily on server-side processing.

The main challenges we faced included:

1. Statelessness: Serverless functions are inherently stateless, which complicated the process of managing OAuth sessions.
2. Cold Starts: The latency introduced by cold starts in serverless functions could potentially disrupt the OAuth flow.
3. Token Management: Securely storing and refreshing OAuth tokens without a persistent server required innovative solutions.
4. Cost Optimization: We had to develop innovative solutions to avoid excessive function calls, as each call came with an associated cost in the serverless model.

Innovative Solutions

To overcome these challenges, we had to think creatively and develop novel approaches:

1. Leveraging Cloud Storage: We used cloud storage solutions to maintain state between function invocations, effectively simulating a stateful environment in a stateless context.
2. Optimizing Function Warm-up: We implemented strategies to keep functions warm, reducing the impact of cold starts on the OAuth flow.
3. Encrypted Token Storage: We developed a secure method of encrypting and storing tokens in cloud storage, ensuring they could be safely retrieved and refreshed as needed.
4. Efficient Function Design: We carefully designed our functions to minimize unnecessary invocations, balancing functionality with cost-effectiveness.

Lessons Learned

This endeavor, though challenging, was an enlightening experience that provided several valuable insights:

1. Deep Understanding of OAuth: The process forced us to understand the OAuth protocol at a fundamental level, beyond just implementing existing libraries.
2. Serverless Capabilities: We gained a profound understanding of the capabilities and limitations of serverless technology.
3. Problem-Solving Skills: The project honed our problem-solving abilities, pushing us to think outside conventional paradigms.
4. Cost-Awareness: We developed a keen awareness of the cost implications of our architectural decisions in a serverless environment.
5. Documentation Importance: The experience underscored the value of comprehensive documentation, inspiring us to document our own process thoroughly for future reference.

Impact on Professional Growth

These experiences not only enriched my technical acumen but also demonstrated my ability to navigate uncharted territories to potential clients. The project became a powerful case study that I could present to showcase my problem-solving skills and adaptability.

Moreover, the knowledge gained from this project positioned me as an early expert in serverless authentication systems. This expertise opened doors to consulting opportunities and speaking engagements, further enhancing my professional profile.

Keeping Up with Technology Trends

In the rapidly evolving world of technology, staying informed about the latest advancements is crucial for any tech professional, especially for freelance developers. My approach to staying current involves a combination of carefully chosen information sources and a commitment to continuous learning.

Key Sources for Tech Trends

- HackerNews
- This Week in Tech (TWiT)
- GitHub trending repositories

Harnessing the Power of HackerNews

One of my go-to resources for staying up-to-date on tech news is Y Combinator's HackerNews. This platform offers a wealth of information about emerging technologies, innovative startups, and current developments in the tech world.

What makes HackerNews particularly valuable is:

1. Community Curation: The upvoting system ensures that the most interesting and relevant content rises to the top.
2. Diverse Perspectives: The comments section often provides insightful discussions and alternative viewpoints.
3. Early Trend Identification: Many emerging technologies and startups are discussed on HackerNews before they hit mainstream tech news.

4. Direct Source Access: Many posts link directly to academic papers, GitHub repositories, or developers' blogs, providing in-depth, firsthand information.

This Week in Tech (TWiT)

For more general tech news, I regularly tune into This Week in Tech (TWiT), a podcast hosted by Leo Laporte. TWiT offers an informed and entertaining perspective on the latest in tech.

My connection with TWiT goes back to my childhood when I was glued to Laporte's shows, 'The Screen Savers' and 'Call for Help' on TechTV. These shows catered to my fascination with computers and were a treat to watch as a young teenager. The nostalgia factor, combined with Laporte's expertise and the show's comprehensive coverage, makes TWiT a reliable and enjoyable source of tech news.

Leveraging GitHub for Technology Trend Insights

In addition to traditional news sources, I've found GitHub to be an invaluable resource for staying current with emerging tools and technologies. By regularly exploring GitHub's trending repositories, tags, and language statistics, I gain real-time insights into what's capturing the developer community's attention.

This approach offers several advantages:

1. Real-time Data: GitHub trends reflect immediate developer interest and activity, often ahead of mainstream tech news.
2. Language and Framework Trends: Observing the rise of certain programming languages or frameworks in GitHub's statistics can indicate shifting industry preferences.

3. Tool Discovery: Many cutting-edge development tools appear on GitHub before they're widely publicized, giving early adopters a significant advantage.
4. Community Engagement: Following trending projects allows me to engage with vibrant developer communities and contribute to open-source initiatives.
5. Quality Assessment: Star counts, fork numbers, and update frequencies provide quick indicators of a project's popularity and maintenance status.

By making GitHub trend analysis a regular part of my routine, I ensure that I'm always aware of the tools and technologies gaining traction in the developer ecosystem. This knowledge not only informs my personal learning path but also allows me to make more informed recommendations to clients, positioning me as a forward-thinking developer in the freelance market.

The Imperative of Continual Learning

The Imperative of Adaptation

The tech industry is defined by constant change and rapid advancement. Being able to adapt to these changes and keeping up with the latest technologies is key to longevity in the field. When I reflect on the trajectory of my career, continuous learning has played a significant role in how it's unfolded.

As a freelancer, I've realized that specializing in older technologies can limit one's prospects. These positions tend to offer lower pay and less interesting work. Moreover, as technologies evolve, demand for specialists in older tech tends to shrink. This is why I am always mindful of where the industry is heading and invest time in learning new technologies that are on the rise.

The Benefits of Staying Current

Staying updated and continually learning doesn't just ensure I remain relevant in the industry, it also opens up exciting new opportunities. By keeping pace with evolving technologies, I've been able to:

1. Work on Innovative Projects: Being familiar with cutting-edge technologies allows me to take on projects that push the boundaries of what's possible.
2. Offer a Broad Range of Services: A diverse skill set enables me to cater to a wider range of client needs.
3. Command Higher Rates: Expertise in in-demand technologies often translates to higher pay rates.
4. Establish Thought Leadership: By blogging about new technologies, I've been able to position myself as a thought leader in certain areas.
5. Enjoy My Work More: Learning new technologies keeps the work exciting and prevents burnout.

Career Advancement Through Continuous Learning and Adaptation

Continuous learning has been a key driver of career progression for me. This commitment to staying current and continually developing my skills has allowed me to ascend from a mid-level developer to senior roles, eventually leading me to a position as a Chief Technology Officer (CTO).

Early Beginnings

My passion for technology started at an early age. At six, I built my first website. From that point, my curiosity took the reins, driving me to continually learn and explore. This unwavering curiosity is a cornerstone of a successful engineer. In this ever-evolving industry, the most successful professionals are those who remain curious, continuously learning, and adapting to the shifting technological landscape.

The Journey to CTO

As I've advanced in my career, my responsibilities and the complexity of the projects I handle have grown. Staying at the forefront of technological innovation has not only facilitated this progression but has also kept me engaged and passionate about my work.

The path to becoming a CTO involved several key steps:

1. Broadening Technical Knowledge: Moving beyond specialization in a single technology to understanding a wide range of systems and how they interact.
2. Developing Leadership Skills: Learning to lead teams, communicate technical concepts to non-technical stakeholders, and drive technological strategy.
3. Understanding Business Impact: Gaining the ability to align technological decisions with business objectives and explain tech investments in terms of ROI.
4. Cultivating a Vision: Developing the capacity to anticipate technological trends and chart a course for the company's technical future.

Throughout this journey, my commitment to learning and my technical blog played crucial roles. The blog served as a platform to solidify my understanding of new concepts, demonstrate my expertise, and connect with other professionals in the field.

A Pivotal Technical Shift

In 2015, I made a critical shift in my go-to tech stack: I moved from PHP (primarily working on WordPress VIP for select clients in the US) to Node.js, catering to new startups and tech agencies. This change was not just a transition between programming languages; it represented a fundamental shift in my career trajectory.

This move propelled me into a new sphere, allowing me to achieve financial independence and providing the freedom to live and work anywhere in the world. The decision to make this shift was driven by several factors:

1. Market Demand: I observed a growing demand for Node.js developers, particularly in the startup ecosystem.
2. Technical Interest: Node.js's event-driven, non-blocking I/O model intrigued me and aligned with my interest in building scalable, real-time applications.
3. Career Growth: The move opened up opportunities to work on cutting-edge projects with innovative startups.
4. Global Opportunities: Node.js's popularity in the startup world meant more remote work opportunities, enabling a location-independent lifestyle.

The TypeScript Transition

One additional significant transition in my career was my early adoption of TypeScript. At the time, TypeScript was a relatively new player in the tech scene. However, I quickly recognized the benefits of static typing from my work with Go, particularly its capacity to facilitate the development of complex applications with numerous components.

The decision to embrace TypeScript early on:

1. Improved Code Quality: Static typing caught many errors at compile-time, reducing runtime bugs.
2. Enhanced Productivity: Better tooling support and autocompletion increased development speed.
3. Better Collaboration: TypeScript's type system made it easier to understand and work with large codebases in team settings.
4. Career Opportunities: As TypeScript gained popularity, my early expertise opened doors to new projects and roles.

This move allowed me to contribute more efficiently to team projects, providing me with another advancement opportunity. It also reinforced the value of being an early adopter of promising technologies.

The Importance of Pivoting and Continuous Adaptation

Unfortunately, I've witnessed colleagues who didn't make such a pivot, clinging to older technologies in the hope of maintaining their positions indefinitely. The harsh reality is that nothing is guaranteed in this industry. Even professionals at top tech companies (the FAANGs: Facebook, Amazon, Apple, Netflix, and Google) are not immune to job cuts.

This observation reinforced my belief in the importance of adaptability. Adapting to the changing technological landscape is not just about survival; it's about thriving in an industry defined by innovation. The tech industry offers limitless opportunities, but to capitalize on them, one must be willing to embrace change, continually learn, and adapt.

Adapting to new technology isn't just about learning new programming languages or systems; it's about a change in mindset. Yes, some individuals might be fortunate to work with the same technology throughout their career. However, the majority of us will need to continually adapt and learn.

In a sense, embracing new technology is a part of our job description. The tech industry is characterized by continuous innovation and change. To advance and thrive, professionals need to mirror this dynamism, continuously learning and adapting to stay at the forefront.

Conclusion: The Power of Curiosity and Adaptation

As we conclude this chapter on my personal blogging journey, it's clear that several key themes have shaped my path in the tech industry. My experience has shown that focusing on niche expertise, particularly in overlooked or emerging technologies, can set you apart in the competitive freelance market. Being an early adopter of promising new tools and frameworks often leads to unique opportunities, while tackling the challenges that come with these cutting-edge technologies not only enhances your skills but also builds your reputation.

Throughout my career, from a curious six-year-old building his first website to a CTO navigating the complex world of modern technology, I've found that continuous learning is crucial for long-term success. Staying informed about industry trends and consistently updating your skill set allows you to pivot when necessary, leading to significant career growth. This willingness to adapt, combined with an insatiable curiosity, has been the driving force behind my professional advancement.

Equally important has been the practice of documenting my journey and sharing knowledge through blogging. This not only helps others in the community but also establishes you as an authority in your field. By contributing to the collective knowledge of the tech community, you position yourself as a valuable resource and thought leader.

As you embark on or continue your own journey in tech, remember that your most valuable asset is your capacity to learn and adapt. Embrace new technologies, share your insights, and never stop being curious. The tech industry rewards those who can navigate change and contribute meaningfully to the community's knowledge base.

In the next chapter, we'll explore practical strategies for growing your blog and building a community around your content, leveraging the experiences and insights we've discussed here.

CHAPTER 4

Overcoming Challenges

The journey of a technical blogger is filled with both rewards and challenges. While sharing knowledge and building a community can be incredibly fulfilling, there are numerous hurdles that every blogger faces along the way. This chapter delves into these challenges, offering insights and strategies to overcome them based on my personal experiences.

From the dreaded writer's block to the complexities of managing long breaks and even considering domain changes, we'll explore the multifaceted nature of maintaining a successful technical blog. We'll also discuss an often-overlooked aspect of blogging: the impact of rest and how changing your environment can boost creativity and productivity.

As we navigate through these challenges, remember that each obstacle is an opportunity for growth. The skills you develop in overcoming these hurdles will not only make you a better blogger but also a more effective communicator and problem-solver in the tech industry.

Overcoming Writer's Block

Writer's block can be a formidable adversary for anyone in a creative field, and technical bloggers are no exception. Despite the fact-driven and research-oriented nature of technical content, the challenge of putting thoughts into words can still be daunting. However, there are several strategies that I've found effective in combating this common issue.

The Power of Continuous Writing

In my experience, the best way to overcome writer's block is, paradoxically, to continue writing. While this might seem counterintuitive, the process of writing – even if it's just jotting down ideas or points you want to discuss – can help unclog the mental pipes.

This approach works because it helps to:

1. Overcome the initial inertia of starting
2. Generate a flow of ideas, even if they're not perfectly formed
3. Create a foundation that you can later refine and polish

I often use a technique I call 'focused free-writing.' This involves setting a timer for a specific period (usually 15-20 minutes) and writing non-stop about the chosen topic. The key is to write without judgment or editing, allowing your thoughts to flow freely. This exercise in momentum forces your brain to make connections and conjure ideas out of necessity, often leading to unexpected and creative solutions.

Changing Your Environment

Another effective strategy I've employed is to change my environment. A new setting can offer a fresh perspective, sparking new ideas and breaking the monotony that might be contributing to the block. This could involve:

1. Working from a different room in your house
2. Visiting a local café or library
3. Taking your laptop to a park or other outdoor space
4. Trying a standing desk or even working while walking on a treadmill

The change in scenery can stimulate your senses and provide new inputs for your brain to process, potentially leading to fresh insights and ideas for your writing.

The Role of Physical Exercise

Physical exercise is not just beneficial, but imperative for clearing the mind and overcoming writer's block. While many find a brisk walk, a short run, or some light yoga helpful, I've discovered that more intense forms of exercise yield better results for me personally. Rigorous exercise, particularly interval training at home, has proven to be the most efficient path in my experience. This type of vigorous physical activity can:

1. Significantly boost blood flow to the brain, enhancing cognitive function
2. Release a potent cocktail of endorphins, dramatically improving mood and motivation

3. Provide a more intense mental break, allowing your subconscious to work on problems more effectively
4. Increase overall energy levels, leading to improved focus and productivity when you return to writing

I've found that a 30-minute high-intensity interval training session can be more beneficial than an hour of light exercise. The short, intense bursts of activity followed by brief rest periods not only improve physical fitness but also seem to "shock" my brain into a more creative state.

Remember, the goal is to find what works best for you. While rigorous interval training has been my go-to solution, the key is to incorporate regular physical exercise into your routine, whatever form that may take for you personally.

Embracing Imperfection

Finally, it's crucial to remember that perfection is the enemy of progress. Your first draft doesn't need to be perfect; it just needs to exist. Once you have something written down, you can refine and polish it.

This mindset shift can be liberating. Instead of pressuring yourself to produce flawless content from the start, give yourself permission to write a "bad" first draft. This approach can help to:

1. Reduce the anxiety associated with starting
2. Get your ideas out of your head and onto the page
3. Provide a foundation that you can later improve upon

Take into account that even the most experienced writers produce drafts that need significant revision. The key is to get started and trust in the editing process.

Taking a Long Break

Every writer needs to take a break at some point. Whether it's for personal reasons, other professional commitments, or simply to recharge, stepping away from your blog for a while is not only acceptable but often necessary. However, managing this break effectively is crucial for maintaining your audience and ensuring a smooth return to blogging.

The Benefits of Taking a Break

Taking a long break from your blog can be a double-edged sword, but when managed correctly, it can provide numerous benefits:

1. Recharging Creative Energy: A break provides the necessary space and time to recharge your creative juices, discover new topics and ideas, and come back to the writing desk with renewed energy.
2. Gaining New Perspectives: Time away from regular blogging can often lead to fresh insights and perspectives. Personally, I find that my most groundbreaking ideas come to me during these times when I'm not actively writing but still subconsciously processing information.
3. Skill Enhancement: In terms of technical blogging, breaks are particularly beneficial because they allow you to acquire new technical skills or deepen your understanding of certain concepts. This not only enhances your writing when you resume but also increases your credibility as a technical blogger.

4. Preventing Burnout: Regular breaks can help prevent burnout, ensuring that you maintain your passion for blogging in the long term.

Managing Reader Expectations

While taking a break can be beneficial for you, it's important to manage your readers' expectations during this period:

1. Communicate Your Plans: If you have a regular posting schedule, communicate your plans to take a break. This helps maintain your relationship with your audience and keeps them engaged with your blog.
2. Provide a Timeline: If possible, provide a rough timeline of your return. This gives your readers something to look forward to and assures them that you're not abandoning the blog.
3. Leave Recommendations: It's a good idea to leave your readers with some recommendations for other blogs or resources to explore in your absence. This shows that you care about their continued learning and engagement, even when you're not actively producing content.

Staying Engaged During the Break

When I decide to take a break from blogging, it's not a complete shutdown. I use this time to explore other blogs, articles, and publications that pique my interest. This exploration and immersion in new content often inspire my own writing when I resume.

Here are some ways to stay engaged during your break:

1. Share Content from Others: While I might not be actively contributing to my blog during these periods, I continue to stay

engaged with my readers through my social media channels. Sharing articles and blog posts from other writers in your field not only helps to fill the gap in content during your break, but it also strengthens your position as a knowledgeable leader in your industry.

2. Engage with Your Network: Use this time to engage with your professional network. Participate in discussions on platforms like LinkedIn or Twitter. This keeps you visible in your field and can lead to new ideas or collaborations.

3. Attend Conferences or Webinars: Use your break to attend industry events. These can be great sources of new information and inspiration for future blog posts.

Returning After a Long Break

Returning after a long break can feel a bit daunting, but remember—it's like riding a bicycle. It might feel strange at first, but soon enough, you'll find your rhythm again. Here are some strategies for easing back into blogging:

1. Start Small: Begin with small, manageable posts to ease back into the routine. This could be a short update post or a quick tutorial on a simple topic.

2. Share Your Journey: Consider writing a post about what you learned or experienced during your break. Your readers might find this interesting and it can help you transition back into regular writing.

3. Plan Ahead: Before fully resuming your blogging schedule, take some time to plan out your next few posts. This can help you feel more prepared and reduce anxiety about consistently producing content.

4. Be Kind to Yourself: Remember that it might take some time to get back to your previous level of productivity. Be patient with

yourself and focus on consistently producing content rather than perfection.

The Impact of Rest on Creativity and Productivity

Taking a break doesn't just offer rest, but can also lead to a fresh burst of inspiration and productivity. For example, during a few "workations" with my wife to the southern beaches of Albania, I found myself inspired to produce a year's worth of top-notch technical articles. The environment, the change of pace, and the novelty of the experience provided the necessary space for my creative energies to flourish.

This experience was so impactful that I eagerly anticipate replicating such breaks in the future. It taught me that sometimes, stepping away from our regular routine can be the best way to reinvigorate our passion for blogging and unlock new levels of creativity.

Deciding to Move to Another Domain

There can be various reasons to consider moving your blog to a new domain. Perhaps you want a domain name that better aligns with your brand or content, you're rebranding, or you've found a domain with better SEO potential. Whatever the reason, this decision should not be taken lightly, as it can have significant implications for your blog's visibility and audience retention.

Reasons for Changing Domains

Before diving into the process of changing domains, it's important to understand the common reasons for making this move:

1. Branding Alignment: Your current domain may no longer reflect your blog's focus or your personal brand.
2. SEO Potential: You might have found a domain that has better keywords or is shorter and easier to remember.
3. Legal Issues: Sometimes, legal challenges or trademark conflicts necessitate a domain change.
4. Consolidation: You might be merging multiple blogs or websites into one.
5. Technical Limitations: Your current hosting situation might be limiting your blog's growth.

In my case, I once considered moving my blog to a new domain to better reflect my evolving focus on more advanced technical topics. The decision process was complex, weighing the potential benefits against the risks of losing some of my established SEO rankings.

Critical Considerations When Changing Domains

The most critical aspect of moving to a new domain is ensuring that your readers can find you. Here are some key considerations:

1. SEO Impact: Understand that a domain change might temporarily impact your traffic and SEO. Google will need to re-index your content under the new domain, which can take time.
2. Redirects: Set up proper 301 redirects from your old domain to your new one. This tells search engines that your site has permanently moved and helps transfer your SEO authority.

3. Update Internal Links: Go through your content and update any internal links to reflect the new domain structure.
4. Inform Search Engines: Use Google Search Console and Bing Webmaster Tools to inform search engines of your site move.
5. Monitor Traffic and Rankings: Keep a close eye on your traffic and search rankings after the move to quickly identify and address any issues.

Keeping Your Audience Informed

Communication is key when changing domains. Here's how to keep your audience in the loop:

1. Announce the Move: Write a blog post explaining the upcoming change, why you're making it, and when it will happen.
2. Email Notifications: If you have an email list, send out notifications about the domain change.
3. Social Media Updates: Use your social media channels to inform followers about the move.
4. Update Profiles: Don't forget to update your domain on all your social media profiles, author bios on other sites, and any other places where your blog is linked.
5. Post-Move Confirmation: After the move, write another post confirming that the change is complete and explaining any actions readers might need to take (like updating bookmarks).

Technical Steps for a Smooth Transition

Here are some technical steps to ensure a smooth transition to your new domain:

1. Choose a Reliable Host: Ensure your new host can handle your traffic and has good uptime.
2. Backup Your Content: Before making any changes, create a full backup of your existing site.
3. Set Up 301 Redirects: These permanent redirects are crucial for maintaining your SEO value.
4. Update Your SSL Certificate: Ensure your new domain has a valid SSL certificate for security.
5. Test Thoroughly: Before announcing the move, test all aspects of your site on the new domain, including functionality, speed, and mobile responsiveness.
6. Gradual DNS Propagation: Be aware that DNS changes can take up to 48 hours to propagate globally. Plan your move accordingly.

My Experience with Domain Changes

In my journey as a technical blogger, I've gone through the process of changing domains twice. The first time was early in my blogging career, and I underestimated the complexity of the process. I lost a significant amount of traffic and it took several months to recover my search rankings.

The second time, I was much better prepared. I meticulously planned every step, from setting up redirects to informing my audience well in advance. This careful planning paid off - the transition was smooth, and I saw minimal impact on my traffic and rankings.

One key lesson I learned was the importance of timing. I chose to make the switch during a typically low-traffic period for my blog, which gave me some buffer to address any issues that arose without significantly impacting my regular readership.

Balancing Work and Play During Workations

The concept of a "workation" - a combination of work and vacation - has gained popularity in recent years, especially in the tech industry. As a technical blogger, I've found workations to be a powerful tool for boosting creativity and productivity. However, striking the right balance between work and leisure can be challenging. Here's what I've learned from my experiences.

Planning Your Workation

Planning a workation can be tricky because you want to make the most out of your time away from the normal routine and environment, yet also remain productive. Here are some key aspects to consider when planning:

1. Choose the Right Location: Look for a place that offers both a stimulating environment and the necessary amenities for work (like reliable internet).
2. Set Clear Goals: Decide what you want to achieve during your workation, both in terms of work and personal experiences.
3. Create a Schedule: Plan your work hours and leisure activities in advance, but be flexible enough to adapt as needed.
4. Pack Appropriately: Ensure you have all the tools you need to work effectively, including any backup equipment, multiple SIM cards, and ensure there's at least 1 café with WiFi close to where you'll be staying.

Setting Boundaries for Work and Leisure

A key aspect of striking the right balance between work and play during a workation is setting clear boundaries for work hours and leisure hours. During my workations in Albania and Italy, I found that scheduling work during the hotter parts of the day, between 11am and 3pm, worked best for me. Here's why this strategy was effective:

1. Optimal Work Conditions: The heat made it uncomfortable to engage in outdoor activities, providing the perfect opportunity to settle down and get work done.
2. Defined Work Period: Having a designated time slot for work ensured that I wasn't working all day and had ample time for relaxation and exploration.
3. Enjoyment of Surroundings: Once the core work hours were over, I dedicated the late afternoons and early mornings to enjoying the picturesque surroundings, going for a swim, and embarking on various trips.
4. Creative Stimulation: This arrangement not only helped maintain productivity but also provided a change of pace that sparked creativity.

Maintaining Productivity in New Environments

Working remotely in a new environment can be challenging initially, but over time, it can lead to significant benefits in productivity and work quality. Here are some strategies I've found effective:

1. Create a Portable Office: Develop a setup that you can easily recreate wherever you are. This might include noise-canceling headphones, a laptop stand, or a portable second monitor.

2. Establish a Routine: Try to maintain some elements of your regular work routine, even in a new environment. This could be as simple as starting your day with a cup of coffee and checking your emails.
3. Use Time Management Techniques: Techniques like the Pomodoro method (working in focused 25-minute blocks) can be particularly useful in maintaining focus in potentially distracting environments.
4. Stay Connected: Ensure you have reliable methods to stay in touch with colleagues or clients. This might mean investing in a portable Wi-Fi hotspot or researching local SIM card options.

Dealing with Distractions

New environments often come with new distractions. Here's how I manage them:

1. Noise Management: I carry two sets of headphones on my workations - USB headphones with a microphone for laptop calls, and earphones with a built-in microphone for phone calls. The latter is particularly effective in isolating noise in noisy environments.
2. Visual Distractions: If you're working in a visually stimulating environment, consider using a privacy screen for your laptop or positioning yourself to face a wall or less distracting view during work hours.
3. Digital Distractions: Use website blockers or apps that limit your social media usage during work hours.
4. Set Expectations: If you're traveling with others, clearly communicate your work schedule to avoid interruptions.

The Impact on Work Quality

Interestingly, I've found that work quality often improves during workations. Here's why:

1. Fresh Perspectives: The change in scenery can provide new insights and approaches to problems.
2. Increased Creativity: Relaxed environments often spark creativity, leading to more innovative solutions.
3. Focused Work Time: The desire to make the most of leisure time can lead to more focused and efficient work periods.
4. Renewed Motivation: The novel experience of a workation can reignite passion for your work, resulting in higher quality output.

Learning from Experience

Over time, working on the road becomes easier, and dealing with distractions becomes second nature. Each workation provides new lessons on how to balance work and leisure more effectively. For those considering taking a workation, it's essential to set boundaries and stick to them. The appeal of a new environment and the joy of vacationing can sometimes blur the lines between work and leisure, leading to either neglecting work or not taking full advantage of the break.

The Unexpected Benefits of Workations

While the primary goal of a workation is to balance work and leisure, I've discovered several unexpected benefits that have significantly impacted my blogging career:

Surge in Creativity and Productivity

During my workations in the southern beaches of Albania, I experienced an unexpected surge in creativity and productivity. The tranquil environment, change of pace from the usual work routine, and the novelty of the experience created a perfect storm for my creative energies.

I found myself brimming with ideas for new blog posts. The inspiration was such that I was able to produce a year's worth of top-notch technical articles, the likes of which I hadn't been able to match since. These articles were not just prolific in quantity, but also rich in quality, covering a range of topics from detailed tutorials and latest technological trends to introspective pieces on the nature of technology itself.

Working in different environments often led me to approach familiar technical concepts from new angles. The change of scenery and routine frequently sparked fresh insights into problems I had previously considered solved. For instance, while working remotely, I found myself reconsidering established patterns in mono-repository architecture. This fresh perspective resulted in a series of articles that resonated deeply with my readers, offering them new ways to understand and implement complex tech concepts.

Cross-Pollination of Ideas

The diverse professional ecosystem of coworking spaces in different cities often led to unexpected connections between tech and other fields. While working alongside a team of engineers and designers in Vancouver, I gained new insights into life as a tech professional in the city that would've otherwise taken years to realize. These unique perspectives, born from international exposure, helped differentiate my blog in the tech space and highlighted the value of diverse work environments in fostering innovation and broader understanding in software development.

Paradoxically, mixing work and vacation taught me valuable lessons about maintaining a healthier work-life balance in my regular routine. I learned to be more efficient during work hours so I could fully enjoy my leisure time, a practice I carried back to my normal work life.

Engaging with Readers During Breaks

Even while on a break or workation, it's crucial to maintain some level of engagement with your readers. Here's how I manage this:

Responding to Comments and Queries

I usually respond to incoming queries directly on the blog itself. The comments section beneath each post is a hive of activity, where readers post their questions, doubts, and sometimes their own insights. Engaging in a dialogue here not only resolves their queries but also deepens the sense of community around the blog.

Direct emails or contacts from readers are less frequent, but when they do come in, they're usually more detailed and specific. Responding to these queries gives me a deeper insight into what my readers are struggling with, and often these interactions lead to ideas for future blog posts.

Social Media Engagement

I must confess that I often struggle with consistently answering queries on social media platforms. The interfaces on these platforms, I find, can be quite distracting, and responding in bulk can be a challenge unless you employ third-party software like Hootsuite. While I do make efforts to engage, I'm not always as responsive as I'd like to be. I've come to realize that managing social media efficiently is a skill in itself, and I have great respect for marketing professionals who navigate these platforms with ease. Despite my shortcomings in this area, I try to balance my social media presence with more direct forms of communication when possible.

However, I do use social media to share interesting articles and insights I come across during my break. This helps maintain a connection with my audience and provides value even when I'm not actively producing new content.

Amplifying Other Voices

During breaks, I aim to amplify other voices in the tech community. Sharing insightful articles or blog posts from different writers can be an excellent way of maintaining engagement with readers. This not only provides fresh perspectives but also fosters a sense of community around shared interests.

When considering voices to amplify, the focus tends to be on innovation and critical perspectives. Personal blogs from respected figures in the tech industry, such as Jeff Atwood's "Coding Horror," often offer valuable insights into programming practices and tech culture. Even comic-based commentary like XKCD, created by Randall Munroe, can provide thought-provoking and often humorous takes on technology and science.

There's also value in sharing major announcements directly from company websites, ensuring information comes straight from the source. While large tech news websites have their place, preference might be given to content that's either directly from the original announcer or offers more in-depth analysis beyond surface-level reporting.

This approach to content curation can serve multiple purposes. It can provide readers with high-quality, authoritative information, encourage critical thinking, and contribute to a more nuanced understanding of tech developments. By carefully selecting content, one can contribute to the larger discourse while offering readers diverse viewpoints that they might not encounter in mainstream tech news.

Conclusion: Embracing Challenges as Opportunities for Growth

From overcoming writer's block to navigating long breaks, considering domain changes, and managing workations, we have explored various challenges associated with technical blogging. At times, these obstacles can seem insurmountable. However, they also present opportunities to learn, grow, and improve our blogging abilities.

The knowledge gained from these challenges makes us not just better bloggers, but better communicators and leaders in the field of technology. Each hurdle we overcome enhances our resilience, creativity, and problem-solving skills - qualities that are invaluable not just in blogging, but in any tech-related career.

As we move forward in our journey as technical bloggers, we must remain adaptable and open to new experiences. From embracing change to overcoming obstacles, every challenge we encounter is an opportunity to evolve and improve. Remember that technical blogging is a journey, and every challenge we overcome is a milestone on the path to becoming better at what we do.

In the next chapter, we'll explore strategies for growing your blog's audience and building a community around your content. We'll discuss marketing techniques, social media strategies, and ways to foster meaningful engagement with your readers. Armed with the resilience and problem-solving skills we've discussed in this chapter, you'll be well-equipped to take on the exciting challenge of expanding your blog's reach and impact.

CHAPTER 5

Growing Your Blog

When I first started my technical blog, I saw it as a solitary pursuit - a place to document my thoughts, experiences, and discoveries in the world of technology. Little did I know that this digital journal would evolve into a vibrant community of like-minded tech enthusiasts, learners, and professionals.

The journey from being a solitary writer to a community builder has been both challenging and rewarding. It's taught me that a successful technical blog is not just about broadcasting your knowledge; it's about fostering connections, encouraging discussions, and creating a space where everyone - from novices to experts - can learn and grow together.

In this chapter, I'll share the strategies and lessons I've learned in growing my blog and building a community around it. We'll dive into the nitty-gritty of SEO, explore the power of social media, and discuss ways to engage with your readers meaningfully. Whether you're just starting or looking to take your established blog to the next level, you'll find practical tips and insights to help you on your journey.

Don't forget, building a community is not an overnight process. It requires patience, consistency, and a genuine desire to add value to your readers' lives. But trust me, the rewards - both personal and professional - are well worth the effort.

Search Engine Optimization (SEO) for Technical Blogs

Understanding How Search Engines Work

Before we dive into the specifics of SEO for technical blogs, it's crucial to understand the basics of how search engines work and address a common misconception. While some argue that SEO is no longer relevant in 2024, the reality is that certain fundamental aspects remain critical for visibility in organic search results.

In simple terms, search engines like Google use automated programs (called bots or spiders) to crawl the web, index content, and rank pages based on hundreds of factors. Even in today's evolving digital landscape, elements such as well-crafted titles and fast-loading web pages continue to play a significant role in how search engines find and rank content.

For us technical bloggers, this means our content needs to strike a balance: it must be valuable to our human readers while also adhering to these basic SEO principles that search engine bots understand. It's a delicate equilibrium, but mastering it can significantly increase your blog's visibility. By focusing on creating high-quality content and ensuring these fundamental SEO elements are in place, you can enhance your chances of being discovered through organic search, even as search algorithms become more sophisticated.

Key SEO Elements for Technical Content

- Optimize titles and meta descriptions
- Use keywords effectively
- Create high-quality content
- Use code snippets and technical diagrams

Key SEO Elements for Technical Content

When it comes to technical content, there are several key SEO elements we need to focus on:

1. Optimizing titles, meta descriptions, and headers: These elements give search engines a quick overview of your content. For technical blogs, it's crucial to include relevant technical terms in these areas. For example, instead of a vague title like "Understanding Web Frameworks," you might use "A Deep Dive into React.js: Features, Performance, and Best Practices."

2. Using keywords effectively without keyword stuffing: Identify the key terms and phrases your target audience is likely to search for. Include these naturally throughout your content, but avoid overusing them. Search engines are smart enough to penalize content that's stuffed with keywords at the expense of readability.

3. Creating high-quality, in-depth content: In the tech world, superficial content rarely cuts it. Search engines favor comprehensive, well-researched articles that thoroughly cover a topic. Don't be afraid to go deep - your readers will appreciate it, and so will search engines.

4. Using code snippets and technical diagrams: These not only make your content more valuable to readers but also signal to search engines that your content is indeed technical in nature.

Technical SEO Considerations

Beyond on-page optimization, there are several technical aspects of SEO that are particularly important for tech blogs:

1. Site speed and mobile optimization: Tech-savvy readers have little patience for slow-loading sites. Optimize your images, leverage browser caching, and consider using a content delivery network (CDN) to speed up your site. Also, ensure your blog is fully responsive and works well on mobile devices.
2. XML sitemaps and robots.txt: An XML sitemap helps search engines understand the structure of your site and find all your content. A robots.txt file tells search engines which pages or sections of your site to crawl or not crawl. Both are especially important for larger tech blogs with complex structures.
3. HTTPS: If you haven't already, migrate your blog to HTTPS. It's a ranking factor for Google, and it's especially important for tech blogs to demonstrate good security practices.

Creating SEO-friendly URLs and Internal Linking Structures

Your URL structure can significantly impact your SEO. For technical blogs, I recommend a structure like this:

```
https://yourblog com/category/post-title
https://yourblog com/web-development/
react-hooks-explained
```

This structure is clean, descriptive, and helps both users and search engines understand the content hierarchy.

Internal linking is another crucial aspect. By linking related posts to each other, you help search engines understand the relationship between your content and provide your readers with easy navigation to relevant information.

Tools for SEO Analysis and Improvement

There are numerous tools available to help you analyze and improve your blog's SEO. Here are a few I've found particularly useful:

1. Google Search Console: This free tool from Google is essential. It helps you monitor your site's performance in search results and identifies issues that might be holding you back.
2. SEMrush or Ahrefs: These paid tools offer in-depth keyword research, competitor analysis, and backlink monitoring. They're not cheap, but the insights they provide can be invaluable.
3. Yoast SEO: If you're using WordPress, this plugin is a must-have. It provides real-time feedback on your content's SEO and readability.
4. PageSpeed Insights: Another free Google tool that analyzes your site's speed and provides specific recommendations for improvement.

Note that these tools are aids, not replacements for quality content. Use them to guide your efforts, but always prioritize creating valuable, informative posts for your readers.

Case Study: How I Improved My Blog's Search Rankings

When I first started my technical blog, I was so focused on creating content that I neglected SEO entirely. As a result, my traffic was minimal, despite the quality of my posts. Here's how I turned things around:

1. Keyword Research: I started by identifying the terms my target audience was searching for. I found that long-tail keywords like "debugging memory leaks in Node.js" performed better than broader terms like "Node.js tips".
2. Content Audit: I went through my existing posts and optimized them based on my keyword research. This involved updating titles, meta descriptions, and headers, as well as expanding some posts to cover topics more comprehensively.
3. Technical Improvements: I migrated my blog to a statically generated website and implemented aggressive caching. This dramatically improved my site speed, which had been a major issue.
4. Internal Linking: I created a system of internal links between related posts, which helped search engines understand the structure of my content better.
5. Regular Posting: I committed to a consistent posting schedule, which helped search engines index my site more frequently.

The results were significant. Within six months, my organic search traffic had increased by 300%, and I was ranking on the first page for several of my target keywords. It wasn't an overnight success, but the steady improvement was incredibly motivating.

Leveraging Social Media for Blog Growth

Social media can be a powerful tool for growing your blog's audience, but it's important to approach it strategically. While these platforms offer great visibility, the key is to use them as a conduit to your blog rather than a final destination for your content. The goal is to leverage social media's reach while ensuring long-term engagement on your own platform. This approach reduces dependency on social media algorithms and protects your content's visibility. In this section, we'll explore how to effectively use social media to boost your blog's visibility and engagement, always with the aim of leading readers back to your home base – your blog.

Choosing the Right Social Media Platforms for Your Niche

Not all social media platforms are created equal, especially when it comes to technical content. After some experimentation, I found that Reddit, LinkedIn, and Twitter were the most effective for my niche. Here's why:

1. Reddit: Subreddits like r/programming and r/webdev are goldmines for sharing technical content, but be careful – Redditors can spot self-promotion a mile away, so focus on providing value.
2. LinkedIn: While it's more formal than Reddit, LinkedIn is excellent for reaching professionals in the tech industry. It's particularly useful for more in-depth, career-focused content.
3. Twitter (aka X): It's where many developers and tech professionals hang out. The fast-paced nature of Twitter is great for sharing quick tips, announcing new blog posts, and engaging in tech discussions.

Strategies for Reddit, LinkedIn, and Twitter

Each platform requires a slightly different approach:

1. Reddit:

    - Become an active member of relevant subreddits before sharing your content
    - Focus on providing value – share your knowledge freely in comments
    - When you do share your content, frame it as a resource, not a promotion

2. LinkedIn:

    - Write LinkedIn articles that complement your blog posts
    - Join and participate in relevant LinkedIn groups
    - Share your experiences and insights, not just your content

3. Twitter:

    - Use relevant hashtags like #WebDev, #JavaScript, or #TechTips
    - Engage in Twitter chats related to your niche
    - Share snippets or key takeaways from your blog posts

Creating Shareable Content for Social Media

The key to social media success is creating content that people want to share. For technical blogs, this often means:

1. Infographics summarizing complex concepts

2. Code snippets solving common problems
3. Quick tips or "TIL" (Today I Learned) posts
4. Polls or questions that encourage engagement

Keep in mind that works on your blog might need to be adapted for social media. A 2000-word tutorial might become a series of tweets highlighting key points, or a LinkedIn carousel summarizing the main concepts.

Building a Consistent Social Media Presence

Consistency is key in social media. It's better to post regularly on one or two platforms than to spread yourself thin across many. Here's what worked for me:

1. Create a content calendar: Plan your social media posts in advance, aligning them with your blog post schedule.
2. Use a social media management tool: Tools like Buffer or Hootsuite can help you schedule posts and maintain a consistent presence without being online 24/7.
3. Engage regularly: Don't just broadcast - respond to comments, participate in discussions, and build relationships.
4. Repurpose content: Turn one blog post into multiple social media posts by highlighting different aspects or insights.

Using Hashtags Effectively

Hashtags can significantly increase the reach of your posts, but they need to be used strategically:

1. Research popular hashtags in your niche: Tools like RiteTag can help you find relevant, active hashtags.

2. Create a mix of popular and niche-specific hashtags: This balances reach with relevance.
3. Don't overdo it: 2-3 hashtags on Twitter, 3-5 on LinkedIn, and 15-30 on Instagram (if you use it) is generally a good rule of thumb.
4. Consider creating a branded hashtag for your blog.

My Social Media Strategy and Its Impact on Blog Growth

When I first started promoting my blog on social media, I made the mistake of simply sharing links to my posts with generic captions. Unsurprisingly, this didn't generate much engagement.

I then developed a strategy I call the "1-on-1-off approach":

- One post featuring highly technical guidance on a new technology.
- One personal post that's lighter in content and value, focusing more on sharing thoughts or anecdotes.

This approach helped me balance technical content with more personal insights, providing a more rounded view of my professional journey and thoughts.

The results were encouraging:

1. Diverse Content: I was able to showcase both my technical expertise and my personality, giving readers a more comprehensive view of who I am as a professional.
2. Improved Engagement: I noticed an increase in interactions on both types of posts, with technical posts garnering professional discussions and personal posts fostering a sense of connection with my audience.

3. Better Work-Life Balance: This approach allowed me to share aspects of my life beyond just technical content, which felt more authentic and sustainable in the long run.
4. Content Variety: The alternating pattern helped me maintain a steady stream of diverse content, keeping my social media presence fresh and interesting.

It's important to stress that building a following doesn't happen overnight. It took consistent effort over several months to see noticeable improvements, but the varied content and interactions I developed made it well worth the effort.

Email Marketing for Bloggers

Despite the rise of social media, email remains one of the most effective ways to connect with your audience. Here's how you could create and grow a thriving newsletter community for your technical blog:

Building an Email List from Scratch

Zero subscribers: where every email marketer begins. Let's explore how to evolve from echoing in emptiness to hosting a virtual tech conference:

1. Offer Valuable, Exclusive Content: Create a comprehensive "Tech Stack Guide" or a "Yearly Tech Trends Report" that's only available to email subscribers. Make sure it's content that truly adds value to your readers' professional lives.
2. Implement Thoughtful Opt-In Placement: Place sign-up forms at natural engagement points - after a particularly insightful blog

post, in your site's footer, or as a slide-in when a reader reaches the end of an article.
3. Leverage Social Proof Authentically: Once you've grown your list, share genuine testimonials from subscribers about how your content has helped them. For example: "Join 5,000+ developers who've used our weekly tips to improve their coding practices."
4. Host Engaging Community Events: Organize online workshops or Q&A sessions with industry experts, requiring email sign-up for participation. This adds immediate value while growing your list.

Creating Compelling Opt-In Offers

Your opt-in offer should be valuable enough that people are willing to exchange their email address for it. Some ideas that worked well for me:

1. Cheat sheets or quick reference guides
2. Video tutorials or mini-courses
3. Exclusive content not available on the blog
4. Access to a private community or forum

Crafting Engaging Newsletters

Once people are on your list, you need to keep them engaged. Here's my approach:

1. Set Expectations: Let subscribers know what they'll receive and how often.
2. Provide Exclusive Value: Include tips or insights not found on your blog.

3. Be Personal: Write as if you're emailing a friend. Share your experiences and thoughts.
4. Keep it Concise: Respect your readers' time. Get to the point quickly.
5. Use a Clear Structure: I typically use this format:

- Personal note or industry insight
- Main content (could be a new blog post, exclusive tip, or curated resources)
- Call-to-action (visit the blog, join a discussion, etc.)

Email Automation and Drip Campaigns

Email automation has been a game-changer for newsletters. It allows you to provide value to your subscribers consistently without manual effort for each email. Here's how you could use it:

1. Welcome Series: New subscribers receive a series of 5 emails over 2 weeks, introducing them to your blog's best content and encouraging engagement.
2. Topic-Based Sequences: Based on the opt-in offer they choose, subscribers are entered into a relevant email sequence. For instance, someone who downloads a "React Hooks Guide" would receive a series of emails diving deeper into React.
3. Re-Engagement Campaigns: For subscribers who haven't opened emails in a while, Send a targeted campaign to rekindle their interest.

Balancing Promotion with Value in Emails

One of the trickiest aspects of email marketing is striking the right balance between promoting your content and providing value. My rule of thumb is the 80/20 principle: 80% value, 20% promotion.

Here's an example of how I structure a typical email:

1. Opening: A personal anecdote or industry insight (value)
2. Main Content: In-depth explanation of a technical concept (value)
3. Related Blog Post: Link to a relevant post on my blog (soft promotion)
4. Community Spotlight: Highlighting a great question or contribution from a reader (value)
5. Closing: Reminder about an upcoming webinar or new course (promotion)

Tools for Email Marketing

There are numerous email marketing tools available. After trying several, I settled on ConvertKit for its ease of use and powerful automation features. However, other popular options include:

1. Mailchimp: User-friendly platform ideal for beginners, with a generous free tier. Offers basic automation, templates, and comprehensive analytics.
2. Drip: Powerful tool for advanced email automation and behavior-driven sequences. Excels in complex segmentation, perfect for sophisticated e-commerce strategies.
3. SendGrid: Robust solution for high-volume email senders with excellent deliverability rates. Provides detailed reporting and easy integration through APIs.

4. AWS SES (Simple Email Service): Enterprise-level email management with granular control and scalability. Ideal for high-volume senders needing detailed analytics and reliable delivery.

GDPR and Other Legal Considerations

As your email list grows, it's crucial to stay compliant with laws like GDPR (General Data Protection Regulation). Here are some key points to remember:

1. Always get explicit consent before adding someone to your list
2. Provide a clear and easy way to unsubscribe in every email
3. Be transparent about how you'll use subscribers' data
4. If you're targeting EU residents, ensure your practices are GDPR compliant

Do note that I'm not a lawyer, so it's always best to consult with a legal professional to ensure you're fully compliant.

Networking and Collaboration in the Tech Blogging Space

Networking has been crucial in growing my blog and expanding my opportunities in the tech space. Here's how I approach it:

Attending and Speaking at Tech Conferences

Tech conferences are goldmines for networking. Here's how I make the most of them:

1. Prepare an "elevator pitch" about your blog

2. Attend talks relevant to your niche and ask thoughtful questions
3. Participate in workshop sessions and hackathons
4. Use the conference app or hashtag to connect with attendees

Speaking at conferences takes this to another level. It positions you as an expert and can drive significant traffic to your blog. Start small with local meetups, then work your way up to larger conferences.

Participating in Online Forums and Communities

Online communities can be great places to share your expertise and subtly promote your blog. I'm active on:

1. Stack Overflow: Answering questions here has led to several loyal blog readers
2. GitHub: Contributing to open-source projects and maintaining my own has been great for networking
3. Dev.to: A supportive community for developers, great for sharing blog posts and engaging in discussions

The key is to focus on providing value rather than overtly promoting your blog. For example, on Stack Overflow, I found that most of my blog's traffic came from users visiting my profile page after reading my helpful answers, without any direct mention of the blog in the answers themselves.

Guest Posting Strategies

Guest posting can expose your writing to a new audience and build valuable backlinks. Here's a potential approach:

1. Identify blogs in your niche that accept guest posts

2. Study their content to understand what topics and styles work well
3. Pitch unique ideas that provide value to their audience
4. Deliver high-quality content that exceeds expectations
5. Promote the guest post as you would your own content

Depending on the industry, aim to do at least one guest post per month. It's a lot of work, but the benefits in terms of exposure and networking are well worth it.

Collaborating with Other Bloggers

Collaboration can take many forms:

1. Co-authored blog posts
2. Joint webinars or online events
3. Podcast interviews
4. Collaborative open-source projects

These collaborations can help you reach new audiences and create content that's greater than the sum of its parts.

Building Relationships with Influencers in Your Niche

Building relationships with influencers can significantly boost your blog's visibility. Here's how I approach it:

1. Start by genuinely engaging with their content (comments, social media interactions)
2. Share their content with your audience, adding your own insights
3. Reach out with specific, valuable opportunities for collaboration

4. Be patient - these relationships take time to develop

Personal Story: How Networking Led to Unexpected Opportunities

Let me share a personal anecdote that illustrates the power of networking in the tech blogging world. A few years ago, I attended a local tech meetup where I struck up a conversation with another attendee about a blog post I'd recently written on optimizing React applications. We had an engaging discussion, and I shared some additional insights that weren't in the post.

Little did I know, this person was a senior engineer at a prominent tech company. A week later, I received an email from him asking if I'd be interested in joining him for a React project they were working on internally. This opportunity not only allowed me to gain more hands-on experience with the local market but also opened my eyes to the potential ahead as a technical consultant. Needless to say, it also enabled me to continue my React writing as I accumulated knowledge.

The lesson here? You never know where a simple conversation might lead. Always be ready to share your passion and expertise – you might just open doors you never knew existed.

Engaging with Your Readers

Building a community around your blog isn't just about attracting readers; it's about engaging with them and fostering a sense of belonging. Here's how I approach reader engagement:

Encouraging and Managing Comments

Comments can transform your blog from a monologue into a dialogue. Here's how I encourage and manage them:

1. End posts with a question or call to action: "What's your experience with this technology? Share in the comments below!"
2. Respond promptly to comments: I aim to reply within 24 hours.
3. Foster discussion: Ask follow-up questions to commenters to keep the conversation going.
4. Moderate effectively: I use a combination of automated spam filters and manual moderation to keep discussions constructive and on-topic.

Responding to Reader Questions Effectively

Reader questions are golden opportunities to provide value and demonstrate expertise. My approach:

1. Answer thoroughly: Don't just give a quick solution; explain the reasoning behind it.
2. Provide context: If relevant, explain how the answer fits into the bigger picture.
3. Include code snippets or examples when appropriate.

4. If the question inspires a longer answer, consider turning it into a full blog post and link to it in your reply.

Creating Polls and Surveys for Reader Input

Polls and surveys are great for understanding your audience better and making them feel involved. I recommend using them to:

1. Gauge interest in potential blog topics
2. Understand my readers' skill levels and interests
3. Get feedback on my blog's content and design

Tools like Google Forms or SurveyMonkey make it easy to create and analyze surveys.

Hosting Q&A Sessions or AMAs

Q&A sessions or "Ask Me Anything" (AMA) events can be powerful engagement tools. I recommend hosting these quarterly, alternating between:

1. Live webinars using tools like Zoom or YouTube Live
2. Reddit AMAs in relevant subreddits
3. LinkedIn Live video streaming events

These sessions not only provide value to your readers but also give you insights into what topics they're most interested in.

Using Reader Feedback to Guide Content Creation

Reader feedback is a goldmine for content ideas. I recommend keeping a running list of:

1. Questions asked in comments or emails
2. Topics requested in surveys
3. Pain points mentioned during Q&A sessions

This list could become the foundation of your content calendar, ensuring that you're always creating content that your audience wants and needs.

Building a Sense of Community Among Your Readers

Creating a sense of community takes time, but it's incredibly rewarding. Some strategies I've found effective:

1. Highlight community contributions: Feature insightful comments or reader projects in your posts or newsletters.
2. Create a forum or Discord server: This gives readers a place to interact with each other, not just with you.
3. Organize community challenges: For example, running a "30 Days of Code" challenge could bring readers together around a shared goal.
4. Encourage reader-to-reader help: When a reader asks a question, invite other readers to share their perspectives before adding your own.

Keep in mind, building a community is about fostering connections – not just between you and your readers, but among the readers themselves.

Content Distribution Strategies

Creating great content is only half the battle; you also need to get it in front of your target audience. Here's how I approach content distribution:

Syndicating Your Content on Platforms like Medium or dev.to

Content syndication can significantly increase your reach. There are several platforms that provide excellent opportunities to attract more readers:

1. Medium: Great for reaching a general tech audience
2. dev.to: Excellent for connecting with other developers
3. LinkedIn Articles: Ideal for more career-focused content

When syndicating, always:

- Wait a week after publishing on your blog (for SEO reasons)
- Include a canonical link to the original post
- Add a note at the beginning indicating where the post was originally published

Using Content Aggregators and Submission Sites

Content aggregators can drive significant traffic to your blog. Some of the platforms I've had success with include:

1. Hacker News: Great for in-depth, technical content. Be prepared for brutally honest feedback!

2. Reddit: Subreddits like r/programming, r/webdev, and r/coding can be goldmines if your content is truly valuable.
3. Lobsters: A community-driven link aggregator for technical content.

Note that these communities often have strict rules about self-promotion. Make sure you're an active participant in the community, not just someone who drops links to their own content.

Creating and Sharing Slide Decks (e.g., SlideShare)

Repurposing your blog content into slide decks can help you reach a different audience. Consider using SlideShare to share decks from conference talks and summaries of more complex blog posts. Some tips:

1. Keep slides visually appealing and not too text-heavy
2. Use plenty of diagrams and infographics
3. Include a clear call-to-action at the end, directing viewers to your blog

Repurposing Blog Content for Different Formats

Different people consume content in different ways. To maximize reach, consider repurposing your blog content into:

1. YouTube videos: Turning tutorial posts into screencasts
2. Podcast episodes: Discussing the main points of a blog post in audio format
3. Infographics: Summarizing key concepts visually
4. Twitter threads: Breaking down a post into a series of tweets

This approach not only reaches different audience segments but also reinforces your message across multiple platforms.

Developing a Content Distribution Calendar

To keep your distribution efforts organized, use a content distribution calendar. Here's a typical timeline for a new blog post:

- Day 0: Publish on blog
- Day 1: Share on social media (Twitter, LinkedIn)
- Day 3: Submit to relevant subreddits
- Day 5: Share in niche Slack communities
- Day 7: Syndicate on Medium and dev.to
- Day 10: Create and share a SlideShare presentation
- Day 14: Record and upload a YouTube video

This approach ensures a steady stream of traffic to each post over time, rather than a single spike on the day of publication.

Analytics and Metrics for Blog Growth

To grow your blog effectively, you need to understand what's working and what isn't. That's where analytics come in.

Key Metrics to Track for Your Blog

While there are countless metrics you could track, I focus on these key indicators:

1. Page Views: How many times your pages are viewed.

2. Unique Visitors: The number of individual people visiting your site.
3. Bounce Rate: The percentage of visitors who leave after viewing only one page.
4. Time on Page: How long visitors spend on each page.
5. Top Traffic Sources: Where your visitors are coming from.
6. Top Performing Posts: Which posts are getting the most views and engagement.
7. Conversion Rate: The percentage of visitors who take a desired action (like subscribing to your newsletter).

Using Google Analytics Effectively

Google Analytics is a powerful tool, but it can be overwhelming. Here's how I use it:

1. Set up custom dashboards for quick access to key metrics.
2. Use the Behavior Flow report to understand how visitors navigate your site.
3. Set up Goals to track important actions (like newsletter sign-ups).
4. Use the Site Speed report to identify and fix performance issues.

Setting Up Goal Tracking and Conversions

Goals in Google Analytics allow you to track specific actions users take on your site. Some goals to track could include:

1. Newsletter sign-ups
2. eBook downloads
3. Contact form submissions
4. Time spent on site (over 3 minutes)

Setting up these goals gives you a clearer picture of how well your site is meeting its objectives.

A/B Testing for Blog Optimization

A/B testing involves creating two versions of a page and seeing which performs better. A/B testing is particularly useful for dedicated funnels rather than individual posts. Here's how you could apply it:

1. Headline Variations: To see which titles attract more clicks.
2. Call-to-Action buttons: Testing different colors, text, and placements.
3. Visual Elements: Compare images, graphics, or layout designs.
4. Form Length: Assess the impact of varying the number of fields.

Tools like Optimizely make it relatively easy to set up these tests.

Creating Data-Driven Content Strategies

Analytics shouldn't just inform your technical decisions; they should also guide your content strategy. Here's how I use data to inform my content creation:

1. Identify top-performing posts and create more content on similar topics
2. Analyze search queries that lead to your site and create content to answer those queries
3. Look at user behavior flow to understand what content keeps readers engaged
4. Use heatmaps (with tools like Hotjar) to see how users interact with your content

My Approach to Using Analytics for Continuous Improvement

I dedicate time each month to dive deep into my analytics. Here's my process:

1. Review key metrics and compare them to the previous month
2. Identify the top-performing and worst-performing posts
3. Analyze why certain posts performed well (or poorly)
4. Use these insights to adjust my content calendar for the coming month
5. Look for technical issues (like slow-loading pages) that need addressing
6. Set specific, measurable goals for the next month

Take into account that the goal isn't just to collect data, but to use it to make informed decisions that improve your blog's performance and better serve your readers.

Building a Personal Brand Through Your Blog

Your blog is more than just a collection of articles; it's a representation of you and your expertise. Building a strong personal brand can set you apart in the crowded tech blogging space.

Defining Your Unique Value Proposition

What makes your blog unique? This is your Unique Value Proposition (UVP). To define a UVP, ask yourself:

1. What specific expertise do you bring to the table?

2. What's your unique perspective on tech topics?
3. What do you offer that readers can't easily find elsewhere?

For example, a UVP for a technical blog might be: "Bridging the gap between cutting-edge AI research and practical implementation for developers." This UVP clearly communicates the blog's focus (web technologies), approach (real-world examples), and special emphasis (performance optimization).

Consistency in Messaging Across Platforms

Once you've defined your UVP, it's crucial to maintain consistency across all platforms. This includes:

1. Your blog
2. Social media profiles
3. Guest posts on other sites
4. Conference talks and webinars

Ensure that your bio, profile pictures, and overall messaging align with your UVP wherever you appear online. This consistent branding helps reinforce your expertise and makes you more memorable to your audience. Consider creating a branding guide for yourself, outlining key phrases, topics, and visual elements that represent your unique value. This guide can serve as a reference point, helping you maintain a cohesive online presence that resonates with your target audience and strengthens your personal brand in the tech community.

Creating a Memorable Blog Design and Logo

Your blog's visual identity is a key part of your brand. I'm not a designer, so I invested in professional help to create:

1. A simple, recognizable logo
2. A consistent color scheme
3. A clean, easy-to-navigate layout

In tech blogging, prioritizing clarity and readability in your design not only ensures your content is accessible and engaging but also helps you stand out and remain memorable across different social platforms.

Developing a Strong About Page and Bio

Your About page is often one of the most visited pages on your blog. Mine includes:

1. A brief professional history
2. My areas of expertise
3. Notable achievements (like leading payments platforms with >100M daily transactions)
4. A personal touch (a nice quote about coding)
5. Clear calls-to-action ("Hire me")

Showcasing Your Expertise Through Case Studies and Portfolios

Demonstrating your expertise goes beyond just writing blog posts. I recommend showcasing:

1. Case studies of successful projects you've worked on.
2. A portfolio of your open-source contributions.
3. Testimonials from clients or readers who've benefited from your content.

These elements add credibility to your brand and give potential clients or employers concrete examples of your skills.

Monetization Strategies (While Maintaining Community Focus)

Monetizing your blog can be tricky. You want to generate income, but not at the expense of your community's trust. Here's how to approach it effectively:

Leveraging Your Blog for Tech Projects

Your blog can be an excellent platform for attracting high-value tech projects. Focus on:

1. Showcasing your expertise through in-depth, problem-solving content.
2. Highlighting case studies of successful projects you've worked on.
3. Demonstrating your thought leadership in specific tech domains.

Creating and Selling Digital Products

Creating your own products can be a great way to monetize your expertise:

1. eBooks: In-depth guides on specific technical topics.
2. Online courses: Video-based tutorials on complex subjects.
3. Code libraries or templates: Time-saving tools for developers.
4. Printable cheat sheets: Quick reference guides for popular frameworks or languages.

When creating these products, focus on solving specific problems for your audience. The key is to identify pain points your readers frequently mention and address them comprehensively.

Offering Consulting or Mentoring Services

Your blog can attract consulting clients. Consider offering:

1. Code review services
2. Performance optimization consulting
3. Technical writing services
4. Career mentoring for developers

Be clear about your areas of expertise and the value you can provide. Dedicate a page on your blog to your consulting services, outlining your process and including testimonials from past clients.

Effective Networking on LinkedIn

Use LinkedIn to amplify your blog's reach and attract professional opportunities:

1. Share your blog posts with insightful comments
2. Engage with other professionals' content in your field
3. Participate in relevant LinkedIn groups
4. Write LinkedIn articles that complement your blog content

Balancing Monetization with Community Value

The key to successful monetization is to always prioritize your community:

1. Be transparent: Always disclose any business relationships clearly.
2. Provide value first: Ensure that your content, whether free or paid, always offers substantial value.
3. Limit promotional content: Stick to a 80/20 rule - 80% pure value, 20% promotional.
4. Listen to feedback: If your community expresses concerns about your monetization strategies, take them seriously.

Don't forget, the trust and goodwill of your community are your most valuable assets. Don't compromise them for short-term gains. By focusing on providing genuine value and showcasing your expertise, your blog can become a powerful tool for attracting high-quality tech projects and consulting opportunities.

Scaling Your Blog's Growth

As your blog grows, you'll face new challenges in maintaining quality and consistency. Here's how you could approach scaling your blog:

When and How to Bring in Guest Authors

Guest authors can bring fresh perspectives and help you publish more frequently, enriching your blog's content diversity. However, it's crucial to approach this strategy thoughtfully. Consider accepting guest posts only when you're consistently receiving high-quality pitches and have established a clear editorial process. This ensures that you maintain the standards your readers expect. Additionally, guest authors can be particularly valuable when you find yourself unable to keep up with the demand for content on your own.

When you decide to incorporate guest authors, it's wise to start with those you know and trust. This approach allows you to refine your collaborative process and maintain quality control before opening up to a wider pool of contributors. As you expand your network of guest authors, you can gradually build a community of experts who contribute to your blog, further enhancing its value and reach.

Strategies for Consistent Content Production at Scale

Maintaining consistency as you scale is crucial. Here are some recommended strategies:

1. Content Calendar: Plan your content at least a month in advance.
2. Batch Creation: Set aside dedicated days for writing multiple posts.
3. Repurposing: Turn one piece of content into multiple formats (blog post, video, podcast).

4. Templates: Create templates for common post types to speed up the writing process.

Building a Team for Your Blog

As your blog grows, you might need to build a team. This could include:

1. Editor: To review and polish posts.
2. Social Media Manager: To handle promotion and engagement.
3. Technical Assistant: To manage the backend of your site.
4. Virtual Assistant: To handle administrative tasks.

Start small and scale your team as your blog's needs (and revenue) grow.

Automating Repetitive Tasks

Automation can save you a lot of time as you scale. Some tasks you could automate include:

1. Social media posting: Using tools like Buffer or Hootsuite
2. Email newsletters: With autoresponder sequences in ConvertKit
3. Comment moderation: Using WordPress plugins to filter spam
4. Analytics reporting: Setting up automated weekly reports in Google Analytics

Balancing Quality and Quantity as You Grow

As you scale, it's tempting to focus on quantity over quality. Resist this urge. Here's how you can maintain quality:

1. Set high standards: Have a checklist for what makes a post "publish-worthy".
2. Get feedback: Use beta readers or a small group of loyal followers to review posts before publishing.
3. Regularly audit your content: Review and update old posts to ensure they remain accurate and valuable.
4. Be willing to publish less: It's better to publish one excellent post than three mediocre ones.

Your reputation depends on the quality of your content. Protect it diligently, as it defines your credibility and drives your growth.

Overcoming Growth Plateaus

Every blog will eventually hit a growth plateau. It's a natural part of the journey, but it can be frustrating. Here's how I've dealt with these plateaus:

Identifying Reasons for Stagnant Growth

When I hit a plateau, the first thing I do is dig into my analytics to understand why. Common reasons I've encountered include:

1. Saturation of current audience
2. Shift in search engine algorithms
3. Increased competition in my niche

4. Stale content strategy
5. Technical issues affecting site performance

Identifying the root cause is crucial for developing an effective strategy to overcome the plateau.

Strategies for Breaking Through Plateaus

Once you've identified the cause, it's time to take action. Here are some strategies that have worked for me:

1. Expand Your Topics: If you've saturated your current audience, consider branching out into related areas.
2. Refresh Old Content: Update and republish your most popular posts with new information.
3. Improve Site Speed: A faster site can lead to better user experience and improved search rankings.
4. Guest Posting: Reach new audiences by contributing to other blogs in your niche.
5. Experiment with New Formats: If you've been focusing on written content, try video or podcasting.
6. Engage More on Social Media: Increase your presence and engagement on platforms where your audience hangs out.
7. Collaborate with Other Bloggers: Joint ventures can expose you to new audiences.

Pivoting Your Content Strategy When Necessary

Sometimes, breaking through a plateau requires a more significant change. I've had to pivot my content strategy a few times over the years. Here's my process:

1. Analyze Current Trends: What topics are gaining traction in your industry?
2. Survey Your Audience: What do they want to learn more about?
3. Assess Your Strengths: What unique perspective can you bring to these new areas?
4. Test New Ideas: Before fully pivoting, test new content types or topics and gauge the response.
5. Gradual Transition: If a new direction is working, gradually increase content in that area while maintaining some of your original focus.

Reinventing Your Blog Without Alienating Existing Readers

When pivoting, it's crucial not to alienate your existing audience. Here's how to manage this:

1. Communicate Clearly: Explain to your readers why you're making changes and how it will benefit them.
2. Maintain Some Continuity: Continue to produce some content in your original niche during the transition.
3. Bridge Old and New: Find ways to connect your new content direction with themes from your existing content.
4. Engage with Your Community: Use surveys, comments, and social media to get feedback on the changes.
5. Be Patient: Give your audience time to adjust to the new direction.

Transforming Community Engagement into Business Opportunities

Building a vibrant community around your technical blog isn't just about fostering discussions; it's a powerful way to create business opportunities. Here's how you can leverage your community engagement to drive professional growth and generate revenue:

Identifying Consulting Opportunities

Your blog's comments section and community forums are goldmines for potential consulting gigs. Here's how to tap into this:

1. Track Common Pain Points: Pay attention to recurring questions or challenges mentioned by your readers. These often indicate areas where your expertise could be valuable in a consulting capacity.
2. Offer Micro-Consulting: For complex questions, consider offering a brief consultation call. This can often lead to larger projects.
3. Create Case Studies: When you successfully help a community member, ask if you can document the process as a case study. This serves as powerful marketing material for your consulting services.
4. Develop Service Packages: Based on common issues in your community, create targeted service packages. For example, if many readers struggle with code optimization, offer a "Performance Audit and Optimization" package.

Developing Products Based on Community Needs

Your community's needs can guide your product development efforts:

1. Conduct Surveys: Regularly survey your community about their biggest challenges and the tools they wish existed.

2. Beta Test with Your Community: When developing a new product, involve your community in beta testing. This not only improves the product but also creates early advocates.

3. Create Ascending Product Levels: Start with free resources, then offer paid products that provide more in-depth solutions. For example:

   - Free blog post on "10 Tips for Securing Your Web Application"
   - Paid eBook on "Comprehensive Web Application Security Guide"
   - Premium video course on "Implementing Advanced Security Measures in Web Applications"

4. Offer Community-Exclusive Deals: Give your community members early or discounted access to your products. This rewards engagement and can boost initial sales.

Networking and Partnership Opportunities

Your community can open doors to valuable professional connections:

1. Identify Potential Partners: Look for community members who offer complementary services or have audiences that align with yours.

2. Facilitate Connections: Use your platform to connect community members with each other. This positions you as a valuable network hub.

3. Organize Virtual Meetups: Host online events where community members can network. This can lead to business opportunities not just for you, but for your community members as well, further increasing the value of your community.

4. Collaborative Projects: Initiate open-source projects or collaborative content creation efforts. These can showcase your leadership skills and lead to high-profile opportunities.

Balancing Monetization and Community Trust

As you explore these opportunities, it's crucial to maintain the trust of your community:

1. Be Transparent: Always be clear about your business relationships and monetization efforts.
2. Prioritize Value: Ensure that any business initiatives provide genuine value to your community.
3. Seek Feedback: Regularly ask your community for feedback on your offerings and adjust accordingly.
4. Give Back: Reinvest a portion of your earnings into the community through improved resources, free events, or supporting community initiatives.

The key to successfully transforming community engagement into business opportunities lies in always putting your community's needs and trust first. By consistently providing value and fostering genuine connections, you create a win-win situation where your business growth aligns with your community's success.

Measuring Community Engagement

To ensure your community-building efforts are effective, it's crucial to measure engagement. Here's how I approach this:

Key Metrics for Community Health

While quantitative metrics don't tell the whole story, they provide valuable insights. Some key metrics I track include:

1. Comments per post
2. Average length of comments
3. Number of returning commenters
4. Time to first response on comments
5. Number of shares on social media
6. Participation rate in community events or challenges

Tools for Tracking Engagement

There are several tools that can help track these metrics:

1. Google Analytics: For overall site engagement metrics
2. WordPress plugins like Comment Analytics: For detailed comment statistics
3. Social media analytics tools: To track shares and discussions on platforms like Twitter or LinkedIn
4. Custom dashboards: I've created my own using Google Data Studio to bring all these metrics together

Using Engagement Data to Inform Your Strategy

Collecting data is only useful if you act on it. Here's how I use engagement data:

1. Identify top-performing posts and analyze why they resonated
2. Spot trends in comment topics to inform future content ideas
3. Recognize most active community members for potential collaboration opportunities
4. Adjust posting schedules based on when engagement is highest
5. Refine community guidelines based on common issues that arise

Balancing Quantitative Metrics with Qualitative Feedback

While metrics are important, they don't capture everything. I also pay close attention to qualitative feedback:

1. The tone and depth of comments
2. Direct feedback from readers via email or social media
3. Testimonials or success stories shared by community members
4. The types of questions being asked in the community

This qualitative data often provides context for the quantitative metrics and can reveal insights that numbers alone miss.

Case Studies: Successful Technical Bloggers

To further illustrate the impact of technical blogging on career advancement, let's look at some successful technical bloggers and the strategies they've employed.

Randall Munroe of XKCD: The Power of Humor

There's something powerfully engaging about humor, especially when it comes to explaining complex technical concepts. Randall Munroe's XKCD comics stand as a beacon of creativity and wit in the tech industry.

Munroe has a unique gift for distilling complex ideas into simple, humorous comic strips that make you laugh and think. His comic on "Standards" (https://xkcd.com/927), released on July 20th, 2011, is a perfect illustration of this talent. In it, Munroe humorously, yet insightfully, points out the cyclical problem of the tech industry's many "global" standards.

Key Takeaways from Munroe's Approach:

1. Simplification: Complex ideas can often be distilled into simple, relatable concepts.
2. Universal Appeal: Humor can make technical content accessible to a broader audience.
3. Memorability: Funny or witty content is more likely to be remembered and shared.

Jeff Atwood of Coding Horror: Changing Perspectives

Jeff Atwood's blog, Coding Horror, has been instrumental in shaping how many developers view their craft. His post "A Programmer's Portfolio" was particularly impactful, changing my perspective on how we, as developers, present our work and ideas.

Atwood emphasized that our work is not just functional but also a form of expression - a showcase of our unique approach to problem-solving, our creativity, and our passion for technology. This realization encouraged me to showcase my work in a different light on my blog.

Key Takeaways from Atwood's Approach:

1. Perspective Shift: Encouraging readers to think about familiar concepts in new ways.
2. Personal Voice: Atwood's posts often include personal anecdotes, making the content more relatable.
3. Thought Leadership: By challenging conventional wisdom, Atwood positions himself as a thought leader in the industry.

Peter Norvig: The Value of Long-Term Perspective

Peter Norvig's article "Teach Yourself Programming in Ten Years" stands in stark contrast to the influx of promises about learning programming in 21 days. Norvig argues that mastery of programming demands significant time and effort, mirroring the 10,000-hour rule of expertise popularized by Malcolm Gladwell.

The appeal of this post isn't just in its audacity to challenge a prevailing notion, but in its honesty about the true effort required to achieve proficiency in programming. This honesty is something I've tried to incorporate into my own blog, not just in discussing the complexity of the subject matter, but also in sharing my personal journey and the evolution of my skills.

Key Takeaways from Norvig's Approach:

1. Honesty: Don't shy away from discussing the true challenges of the field.
2. Long-term View: Encourage readers to think about their career in terms of years, not weeks or months.
3. Depth Over Speed: Emphasize the importance of deep understanding over quick, surface-level knowledge.

The Impact of Community Platforms on Technical Blogging

HackerNews: Raising the Bar

The culture at HackerNews has certainly held me to a higher standard when it comes to tech blogging. The audience there is sophisticated and well-informed, making them a challenging yet rewarding group to write for. They value solid, well-reasoned ideas and are quick to critique any that lack depth or substance.

This has forced me to exercise thoroughness in my research and clarity in my writing. Every blog post undergoes several rounds of verification and refinement before it sees the light of day. This attention to detail, although time-consuming, has helped me create content that stands up to scrutiny and offers real value to my readers.

Reddit: A Mixed Bag of Insights

Reddit has influenced my perspective as a tech blogger to a somewhat lesser extent. The subreddit communities can be a rich source of deep-dive discussions and unique insights. However, finding these gems among the increasing volume of content has become more challenging.

Despite some concerns about moderation issues, Reddit remains a valuable source of inspiration and learning. Moreover, these challenges highlight an opportunity for innovative minds looking to disrupt the status quo in online communities.

Conclusion: The Ongoing Nature of Community Building

As we wrap up this chapter on growing your blog and building a community, it's important to remember that this is an ongoing process. Building a thriving community around your blog doesn't happen overnight – it requires consistent effort, patience, and a genuine commitment to providing value to your readers.

Throughout this exploration of successful bloggers and communities, we've learned that:

1. Community building is a marathon, not a sprint. It takes time to cultivate a loyal and engaged readership, as exemplified by long-standing blogs like XKCD and Coding Horror.
2. Flexibility is key. What works today may not work tomorrow, so always be ready to adjust your strategies based on your audience and the community you're engaging with.

3. Your community is your greatest asset. Nurture it, listen to it, and let it guide your blog's evolution, just as platforms like HackerNews can push you to higher standards.
4. Authenticity and a unique perspective matters. Whether it's Randall Munroe's humor or Peter Norvig's long-term view, your unique voice and genuine passion for your subject will attract like-minded individuals and form the core of your community.
5. Continuous learning and improvement are essential. The blogging landscape is always changing, so stay curious and open to new ideas, technologies, and platforms.

Embracing Your Role as a Community Leader

As your blog grows and your community develops, you'll find yourself transitioning into a role that's part educator, part moderator, and part community leader. Embrace this role. Your blog is no longer just about broadcasting your knowledge – it's about facilitating learning, fostering connections, and creating a space where ideas can flourish.

Remember that your influence extends beyond just the content you create. Your actions, your responses to comments, and the overall culture you cultivate on your blog all contribute to shaping your community. The standards set by platforms like HackerNews can serve as a benchmark for the quality and depth of discussions you aim to foster.

As you move forward, continue to challenge yourself. Experiment with new content formats, explore emerging technologies, and always strive to provide more value to your community. But most importantly, enjoy the journey. Building a community around your passion for technology is one of the most rewarding aspects of technical blogging.

In the next chapter, we'll explore how technical blogging can become a powerful catalyst for your professional growth. We'll delve into the ways consistent blogging can enhance your visibility in the tech industry, open doors to new opportunities, and accelerate your career progression. From landing major projects to establishing direct connections with decision-makers, you'll discover how your blog can become much more than just a platform for sharing knowledge – it can be a transformative tool for your entire career trajectory. Get ready to unlock the full potential of your technical blog as we examine its profound impact on professional development in the ever-evolving tech landscape.

CHAPTER 6

The Impact of Blogging on Your Career

In the ever-evolving landscape of technology, the way we present ourselves professionally has undergone a significant transformation. No longer confined to traditional resumes and business cards, our digital presence has become a powerful tool for career advancement. This chapter delves into how technical blogging can profoundly impact your career trajectory, opening doors to opportunities you might never have imagined.

As we explore this topic, we'll draw from my personal experiences and those of other successful technical bloggers, examining how consistent documentation of our technical journeys can lead to professional growth, enhanced visibility, and exciting new prospects in the tech industry.

The Digital Evolution of Professional Networking

From Paper to Pixels: The Digital Business Card

Years ago, in a move that merged technology with self-presentation, I dedicated a subdomain of my website to serve as a digital business card. This innovation, born out of the digital age, was a departure from the traditional paper and ink to an online, living representation of myself. Equipped with bilingual capabilities in English and German, it ensured a wider reach in our globalized tech world.

Although I haven't updated this digital business card in a while, it remains an enduring testament to the potential of tech-savvy self-promotion. Its creation was an early indicator of how our professional identities could be shaped and presented in the digital realm.

The digital business card, with its concise profile, portfolio of experiences, and multiple contact options, provided a streamlined way to network. It proved invaluable at industry events and meetups where physical business cards often ran out or were forgotten. Its omnipresence meant that anyone, anywhere could access my professional information, making it an indispensable tool in my networking endeavors.

The Blog as a Professional Home Base

While the digital business card was an innovative networking tool, my blog has served an even more crucial role in my career development. It has been more than just a platform for showcasing innovations or disseminating information. Instead, it has become a constant, a home base amidst the whirlwind of technological advancements and shifting career landscapes.

This digital chronicle has captured the nuances of my learning, the milestones of my career, and my reflections on the industry's seismic shifts. It's been my own piece of the digital universe, a personal repository that not only contains my work and thoughts but also mirrors my growth as a technologist.

The practice of consistent, reflective documentation has been integral in reinforcing my learnings, providing a visible record of my technical evolution, and presenting a roadmap of my career progression. It's a tangible demonstration of my commitment to continuous learning and my ability to articulate complex technical concepts – skills highly valued in the tech industry.

Blogging as a Learning Tool

The Django Journey: A Case Study in Learning Through Blogging

When I embarked on learning Django, I made a conscious decision to document my journey publicly. This wasn't merely to display my understanding of Django; it was an intentional strategy to embed a culture of consistent documentation into my learning process.

I wrote about the nitty-gritty details, the highs and lows, the complexities and triumphs. As my understanding grew, I even developed a significant open-source library based on my learnings. This public documentation was more than just an exercise in understanding Django better; it was a structured effort to create a culture of learning deeply intertwined with consistent documentation and sharing.

By making my learning process visible and tangible, I not only cemented the knowledge in my own mind but also created a valuable resource for others exploring the same territory. This approach exemplifies the power of learning in public – it benefits both the learner and the wider tech community.

The Emacs Configuration Odyssey

Another standout example of how blogging enhanced my learning is my exploration of Emacs configuration. For years, I'd been trying to develop a lean version of Spacemacs that included only org-mode and some basic shortcuts. This challenging task required grappling with intricate details and devising unique solutions.

Throughout this process, I kept detailed records of my progress, documenting each step, challenge, and victory on my blog. This disciplined approach to learning not only deepened my understanding of the subject but also created a valuable learning resource for others exploring the same territory. Importantly, this journey significantly optimized my main tool for writing both notes and blog posts, making my entire workflow more efficient and tailored to my needs.

This experience reinforced my belief that learning isn't a solitary pursuit. By sharing my journey, I was able to contribute to a broader community of learners, adding another dimension to my professional growth. The feedback and discussions generated by these posts often led to new insights and further improvements in my configuration. Moreover, the process of documenting and sharing my Emacs customization not only helped others but also pushed me to refine and perfect my writing environment, demonstrating how blogging can directly improve the tools we use in our daily work.

Blogging as a Career Catalyst

Landing Major Projects Through Blogging

Perhaps the most significant win in my career resulting from my blogging activities was landing a project for a major national company. This opportunity was transformative, propelling me to the forefront of significant projects and establishing me as a credible figure in the industry.

My blog, with its depth of technical posts and reflections on the industry, was instrumental in securing this opportunity. It served multiple purposes:

1. Demonstrated Expertise: The technical depth of my posts showcased my knowledge and skills in a way that a resume alone never could.
2. Proven Communication Skills: My ability to explain complex concepts clearly through my blog posts was a key factor in the company's decision.
3. Showed Commitment to Learning: The regularity of my posts and the range of topics covered demonstrated my commitment to continuous learning and staying current with industry trends.
4. Provided a Body of Work: My blog served as an extensive portfolio, giving the company insight into my thought processes and problem-solving approaches.

The visibility and credibility that blogging provided were key factors that set me apart from other candidates and helped me secure this pivotal role. It's a clear example of how technical blogging can open doors to opportunities that might otherwise be out of reach.

Career Advancements Through Blogging

- Landed projects with major companies
- Secured consulting roles
- Transitioned to CTO positions

From Blogger to Consultant: The AngularJS Experience

Another instance where my blog directly impacted my career was when my in-depth posts on AngularJS led to a consulting role with a major airline. This experience highlighted how specialized knowledge, when shared effectively through a blog, can create unique career opportunities.

My series of posts delved into the intricacies of AngularJS, covering everything from basic concepts to advanced techniques and best practices. These articles served as a comprehensive resource for developers working with AngularJS, filling a gap in the existing documentation.

The impact of these posts was two-fold:

1. Established Expertise: The depth and breadth of my AngularJS content positioned me as an expert in the field.
2. Demonstrated Problem-Solving: By addressing common issues and providing solutions, I showcased my problem-solving skills and practical approach to development.

When the airline was looking for an AngularJS consultant, my blog served as a testament to my expertise and ability to communicate complex ideas clearly. This increased visibility and credibility within the tech community played a crucial role in landing the consulting role, proving once again the powerful impact of technical blogging on career advancement.

It's worth noting that these AngularJS posts remain some of my most popular content to date, even years after their initial publication. This enduring popularity underscores the long-term value of creating high-quality, in-depth technical content. It demonstrates that well-crafted blog posts can continue to attract readers, establish your expertise, and open up opportunities long after they're written, serving as a lasting testament to your knowledge and skills in the tech community.

The MEAN.js Deep Dive: Unexpected Collaborations

While exploring the MEAN.js stack, I wrote a series of articles explaining the intricacies of the technology. My deep dive into the framework was meant to provide developers with a comprehensive resource to understand and leverage MEAN.js effectively.

Unexpectedly, these articles not only resonated with the tech community but also caught the attention of the actual developers of the MEAN.js framework. The quality and depth of the content impressed them enough to reach out to me directly for potential collaboration.

This experience highlighted several important points:

1. Far-Reaching Impact: Our efforts to share knowledge can have a much broader impact than we initially imagine.
2. Recognition from Peers: When our work is recognized by the very people who developed the technology we're writing about, it's a powerful validation of our expertise.
3. Opening New Doors: While I ultimately couldn't accept their offer due to relocation constraints, this interaction opened up a dialogue with the core developers and expanded my professional network.
4. Value of Comprehensive Content: The series, consisting of five in-depth pieces, highlighted the importance of creating thorough, detailed resources for developers.

This interaction reinforced the idea that technical blogging could be a powerful platform for connecting with like-minded professionals and organizations in the tech industry. It showed that by consistently producing high-quality, in-depth content, we can attract opportunities for collaboration and professional growth.

From Tech Writer to FinTech CTO: Leveraging Blog Expertise

My journey into the upper echelons of FinTech leadership is a testament to the power of consistent, focused blogging. As I increased my writing on FinTech and payment systems, I unknowingly laid the groundwork for a significant career leap.

The FinTech industry, particularly in Switzerland, is known for its rigorous standards and competitive landscape. Leadership positions in this sector are highly coveted and typically require years of specialized experience. However, my extensive body of work on FinTech topics served as a powerful portfolio, demonstrating not just knowledge, but deep insights into the industry's challenges and trends.

My blog posts on topics like FinTech, regulatory technology (RegTech), and the evolution of payment systems caught the attention of a Swiss FinTech startup. These articles showcased not only my technical knowledge but also my understanding of the broader financial ecosystem and regulatory landscape - crucial aspects for a leadership role in FinTech.

The transition to CTO of this startup was a direct result of the expertise I had cultivated and shared through my blog. It allowed me to bypass traditional career ladders and prove my capabilities in a way that a resume alone never could. This experience underscores the potential of technical blogging to open doors to leadership roles, even in highly competitive and specialized industries.

Advice for Aspiring FinTech Leaders:

1. Focus on Interdisciplinary Knowledge: FinTech is at the intersection of finance and technology. Write about both aspects and how they interact.
2. Stay Current with Regulations: The financial industry is heavily regulated. Demonstrating your understanding of regulatory challenges can set you apart.
3. Analyze Trends: Don't just report on new technologies; analyze their potential impact on the industry.
4. Showcase Problem-Solving: Write about real-world FinTech problems and your proposed solutions.
5. Engage with the Community: Participate in FinTech forums and comment on others' work to build your network.

Remember, transitioning into a leadership role isn't just about technical knowledge. Use your blog to demonstrate your vision for the industry, your ability to simplify complex concepts, and your understanding of business strategy. These skills are crucial for a CTO role and can be effectively showcased through thoughtful, well-written blog posts.

Cloud Expertise to DevOps Leadership: The Power of Shared Knowledge

Another significant career transition facilitated by my blog was my move into DevOps leadership roles and increased involvement with enterprise-level projects. This shift was largely driven by my consistent writing about cloud orchestration and automation.

As cloud technologies evolved, I made it a point to document my experiences, challenges, and solutions in implementing and optimizing cloud infrastructures. These posts ranged from practical tutorials on setting up complex cloud environments to thought pieces on the future of cloud computing and its impact on business operations.

My articles on topics like multi-cloud strategies, containerization, and Infrastructure as Code (IaC) demonstrated not just technical proficiency, but also a strategic understanding of how these technologies could be leveraged to solve business problems. This combination of technical depth and business acumen is particularly valuable in DevOps roles, where bridging the gap between development and operations is crucial.

The visibility gained through these posts led to multiple DevOps leadership positions over the years. More importantly, it opened doors to contracting opportunities with large enterprises - a notoriously difficult market to break into as an individual contractor. Enterprises, often risk-averse and preferring established relationships, were willing to engage based on the expertise demonstrated in my blog.

This transition highlights how consistent, high-quality blogging can not only showcase your technical skills but also position you as a thought leader capable of driving organizational change. It proves that sharing knowledge freely can lead to valuable opportunities, even in the most challenging and competitive areas of the tech industry.

Advice for Aspiring DevOps Leaders:

1. Document Real-World Scenarios: Share your experiences with actual cloud and DevOps implementations, including challenges faced and how you overcame them.

2. Explore Cutting-Edge Tools: Regularly write about new DevOps tools and methodologies, demonstrating your commitment to staying current.
3. Emphasize Business Impact: Don't just focus on the technical aspects; discuss how DevOps practices can improve business outcomes.
4. Cultivate a Holistic View: Write about the entire software development lifecycle, showing your understanding of how DevOps fits into the bigger picture.
5. Share Automation Scripts and Templates: Provide practical resources that others can use, establishing yourself as a go-to resource in the community.
6. Discuss Cultural Aspects: DevOps is as much about culture as it is about technology. Share insights on fostering a DevOps culture in organizations.

When aiming for enterprise contracts, use your blog to demonstrate not just your technical skills, but also your understanding of enterprise-scale challenges. Write about topics like compliance, large-scale migrations, and integrating DevOps in traditional corporate structures. This shows that you can operate effectively in enterprise environments.

Remember, consistency is key. Regular, high-quality posts build trust and demonstrate dedication to your field. Over time, this establishes you as a thought leader, making you an attractive candidate for leadership roles and lucrative contracts.

By sharing your knowledge generously and consistently, you're not just building your personal brand - you're contributing to the broader tech community while opening doors to exciting career opportunities.

A Direct Line to Decision Makers

One of the most significant benefits of my technical blogging journey has been the direct line of communication it has established with tech leads and recruiters. Instead of navigating the often-tedious process of HR filtering, my blog has served as an authentic showcase of my skills and expertise, attracting the attention of the very people making hiring decisions.

This direct connection has several advantages:

1. Bypassing Gatekeepers: My blog allowed me to circumvent traditional recruitment procedures and engage directly with hiring managers.
2. Showcasing Real-World Skills: Through my blog posts, I could demonstrate not just theoretical knowledge, but practical application of skills in real-world scenarios.
3. Proving Communication Abilities: Technical blogs showcase not just coding skills, but also the crucial ability to explain complex concepts clearly – a vital skill in many tech roles.
4. Demonstrating Passion and Initiative: Regular blogging shows a level of passion for technology and initiative in continuous learning that's hard to convey in a traditional resume.

By serving as a comprehensive portfolio of my work, thoughts, and skills, my blog has repeatedly opened doors to new opportunities, often allowing me to skip several steps in the traditional hiring process.

The Power of Sharing Technical Solutions and Portfolio Building

The GitHub Account Management Saga

One particularly impactful blog post came from my struggle with managing multiple GitHub accounts across different repositories. This common challenge among developers led me on an intense learning journey, filled with trial and error, numerous configurations, and much deliberation.

The goal was to figure out how to use .ssh/config and eventually .gitconfig to manage different accounts seamlessly. The eureka moment came when I realized that the right .gitconfig configuration could automate the entire setup, eliminating the worry over different SSH keys.

Recognizing the universal relevance of this challenge, I decided to document the entire process on my blog. I detailed each step of my journey, from the initial struggles to the eventual resolution, creating a comprehensive guide for developers facing similar issues.

The impact of this post was significant:

1. Community Resonance: The blog post resonated with many developers facing similar challenges, generating a lot of engagement and discussion.
2. Demonstrating Problem-Solving: It showcased my ability to tackle complex, real-world problems and find effective solutions.
3. Knowledge Sharing: By breaking down the process into digestible, actionable steps, I was able to help others overcome this common hurdle.

4. **Establishing Credibility**: Successfully solving and explaining a widespread issue bolstered my credibility in the developer community.

This experience reinforced the value of sharing knowledge within the tech community and highlighted how even seemingly niche problems can lead to widely appreciated content.

WordPress Expertise: A Tangible Demonstration of Skills

While blogging has been a primary means of showcasing my expertise, I've also found success in demonstrating my skills through other tangible projects. A prime example of this is my work with WordPress.

Over the years, I developed numerous WordPress websites and plugins. This body of work served as concrete evidence of my skills, playing a significant role in landing me an interview with a prominent WordPress VIP company.

The key takeaways from this experience were:

1. **Practical Demonstration**: My WordPress sites and plugins provided a practical demonstration of my coding abilities, design sensibilities, and problem-solving skills.
2. **Breadth of Skills**: The variety of plugins in my portfolio showcased my ability to tackle diverse challenges within the WordPress ecosystem.
3. **Long-Term Commitment**: My continued work with WordPress demonstrated a long-term commitment to and deep understanding of the platform.
4. **Open Source Contribution**: Many of my WordPress projects were open source, showing my ability to work collaboratively and contribute to the wider developer community.

This experience reiterated that showcasing your work in a publicly accessible manner, whether through blogging or portfolio websites, can significantly boost your visibility and career prospects in the tech industry.

Conclusion: The Transformative Power of Technical Blogging

As we've explored throughout this chapter, technical blogging is far more than a hobby or a side project - it's a powerful career accelerator that can transform your professional trajectory in ways you might never have imagined.

We've seen how blogging serves as an unparalleled learning tool, from mastering Django to optimizing Emacs configurations. The act of writing solidifies your understanding and creates a valuable resource for others, establishing a virtuous cycle of learning and teaching.

More importantly, we've witnessed the incredible career-catalyzing potential of consistent, high-quality blogging. From landing major projects and consulting gigs to opening direct lines of communication with decision-makers, a well-maintained blog can bypass traditional career gatekeepers and showcase your expertise in ways a resume never could.

The journey from tech writer to FinTech CTO and the transition into DevOps leadership roles stand as testament to the doors that technical blogging can open. These examples demonstrate how sharing your knowledge can position you as a thought leader, even in highly competitive and specialized fields.

We've also seen how sharing solutions to common technical challenges, like managing multiple GitHub accounts or creating WordPress plugins, can establish your credibility in powerful ways.

The key lessons from this chapter are clear:

1. Blogging as a Learning Tool: The act of writing about what you learn reinforces your understanding and creates valuable resources for others.
2. Career Catalyst: Your blog can attract opportunities, bypassing traditional hiring processes and connecting you directly with decision-makers.
3. Building Authority: Consistent, high-quality blogging can establish you as an expert in your field.
4. Your blog is your portfolio - make it a showcase of your skills and thought processes.
5. Engage with your community - the connections you make through blogging can lead to unexpected opportunities.

As you embark on or continue your technical blogging journey, remember that each post is a step towards greater opportunities. Your blog is not just a collection of articles - it's a powerful tool for career advancement, a platform for continuous learning, and your unique contribution to the tech community.

CHAPTER 7

My Personal Blogging Journey

As I reflect on my journey through the world of technology and blogging, I'm struck by how intertwined these two paths have been. From my earliest forays into web development to my current role as a high-end Fractional CTO and Tech Lead, my commitment to documenting and sharing my experiences has been a constant thread, weaving through every stage of my career. This chapter is a testament to the power of technical writing, not just as a means of sharing knowledge, but as a catalyst for personal and professional growth.

The Early Days: A Tech News Website in Junior High

My journey into the world of technical blogging began earlier than most. In 2004, while still in junior high, I embarked on an ambitious project that would set the course for my future career. I created a tech news website, rallying a group of friends to each contribute a weekly article. This wasn't just a school project or a passing fancy; it was my first real foray into managing a digital platform and creating content.

The website was built using PHPNuke, which at the time was cutting-edge technology. Looking back, I'm amazed at the audacity of my younger self. Here I was, barely a teenager, grappling with content management systems, web hosting, and the logistics of running a collaborative online platform. Little did I know that this early experience would prove invaluable in my future career.

Managing this website taught me more than just the technical skills of web development. It was a crash course in content creation, team management, and the importance of consistent output. These were lessons that would serve me well throughout my career, forming the foundation of my approach to technical leadership and project management.

From PHPNuke to Professional Recognition

The skills I developed while building and customizing my PHPNuke-based website didn't just remain a hobby. They became the key that unlocked my first professional opportunity. During my first job interview, I was able to demonstrate a level of technical proficiency that set me apart from other candidates. This wasn't just theoretical knowledge gleaned from textbooks; it was practical, hands-on experience that I could articulate clearly.

What struck me most about this experience was the realization that I was competing for a position typically filled by individuals a decade older than me. My early start in web development and technical writing had given me a significant advantage. It wasn't just about knowing how to code; it was about understanding systems, problem-solving, and being able to communicate technical concepts effectively.

This early success was a powerful affirmation of the value of hands-on experience and the importance of documenting one's learning journey. It set a pattern that I would follow throughout my career: learn, apply, document, and share.

The WordPress Years and a Bold Move to Germany

As my skills evolved, so did my choice of platforms. I transitioned from PHPNuke to WordPress, a move that would prove significant in my career. Throughout this transition, I maintained my habit of thoroughly documenting my learning process. Every new feature I discovered, every challenge I overcame, found its way into my blog posts. Little did I know how crucial this documentation would become.

In a bold move that would test both my personal resilience and professional capabilities, I decided to relocate to Germany. I arrived with nothing more than a backpack and a vague plan of what I wanted to achieve. It was a leap into the unknown, but I was armed with my skills, my experience, and most importantly, my documented journey of learning and problem-solving.

The power of my technical writing became apparent almost immediately. Within three days of arriving in a new country, I secured a job interview and a subsequent offer. The interviewer was impressed not just by my technical skills, but by the breadth and depth of knowledge demonstrated in my blog posts. My writing served as a portfolio, a testament to my abilities and my commitment to continuous learning.

This experience hammered home a crucial lesson: in the fast-paced world of technology, your ability to learn and adapt is often more valuable than your current knowledge. By documenting my learning journey, I had unknowingly created a powerful tool for demonstrating this ability. It wasn't just about showcasing what I knew, but about illustrating my capacity to tackle new challenges and quickly come up to speed on new technologies.

The job offer that followed was more than just employment; it was validation of my approach to learning and sharing knowledge. It reinforced my belief in the power of technical blogging, not just as a means of helping others, but as a tool for personal and professional growth.

The Google Grant and a Lesson in Cloud Security

A few years into my career in Germany, I experienced a significant breakthrough that would further cement the importance of technical writing in my journey. I developed a Python-based data aggregation software, initially created as an event collection library for a Berlin-based event app. As I built robustness into the tool, I realized its potential as a standalone data aggregation software.

Seizing an opportunity, I entered a competition at the local Google Berlin branch. The result was beyond my expectations - I was awarded a substantial Google Cloud credit grant of $20,000. This was a pivotal moment, validating my work and opening up new possibilities.

Excited by this windfall, I decided to migrate all my blogs and websites to Google Cloud. The migration process was tedious but rewarding, and I went to bed that night feeling accomplished. However, the next morning brought a rude awakening - none of my websites were working. It turned out that the Google IP ranges were under heavy attack at the time, and within just 10 hours, my systems had been hacked.

This could have been a devastating setback, but I chose to see it as an opportunity. Drawing on my habit of documenting my experiences,

I wrote a comprehensive article about the migration process and the subsequent hack. This article, born out of adversity, became one of my most-read pieces to date.

The incident and the resulting article taught me several valuable lessons:

1. The importance of security in cloud environments.
2. The value of turning setbacks into learning experiences.
3. The power of transparency in technical writing.
4. The enduring interest in real-world tech experiences, especially when things go wrong.

This experience reinforced my belief in the value of sharing not just successes, but also failures and challenges. It demonstrated that readers appreciate honesty and real-world experiences, and that even negative incidents can be turned into valuable content.

Scaling the Career Ladder: From Full Stack Developer to a Global Tech Lead

My commitment to continuous learning and documentation continued to pay dividends as my career progressed. I spent several successful years as a Full Stack developer at a leading agency, working with major clients such as Germany's largest news agency and Switzerland's largest retailer. During this time, I not only honed my technical skills but also developed my ability to communicate complex concepts, often giving seminars to technical teams about various technologies.

The next significant leap in my career came when I leveraged my years of WordPress experience to secure a remote position with a WordPress

VIP company based in New York City. This was a major breakthrough on multiple fronts:

1. It doubled my salary, validating the market value of my skills and experience.
2. It proved that I could work effectively in a fully remote capacity.
3. It elevated my work to international standards, allowing me to contribute to the very core of WordPress technology.

This transition felt like a graduation of sorts - from working on a national level, to a regional level, and finally hitting the global stage. It was a point of no return; I knew I wouldn't go back to working solely on a regional scale after this.

The role challenged me to elevate my skills even further. Working with a distributed team across different time zones, I had to refine my communication skills and adapt to asynchronous workflows. My habit of thorough documentation proved invaluable in this context, allowing me to contribute effectively despite the physical distance from my colleagues.

This period of my career underscored the importance of not just having technical skills, but being able to demonstrate them clearly. My blog posts and technical articles served as a portfolio, showcasing not just what I knew, but how I thought and problem-solved. It was a testament to the power of technical writing in opening doors and creating opportunities.

Pivoting to Leadership: The Journey to CTO

My transition from a hands-on developer to a leadership role was a significant milestone in my career, heavily influenced by my continuous learning and documentation practices. After years of successful remote consulting, I made a strategic decision to pivot towards Node.js and, to a lesser extent, Django. This move was driven by my constant monitoring of industry trends and a commitment to keeping my skills relevant in an ever-evolving market.

The Node.js Transition

The decision to focus on Node.js wasn't made lightly. I spent months researching, experimenting, and gauging the direction of the industry. As always, I documented parts of this journey on my blog. I wrote about my initial struggles with asynchronous programming, my experiments with various Node.js frameworks, and my thoughts on how Node.js compared to other technologies I'd worked with.

One pivotal project that cemented my appreciation for Node.js was developing a proof of concept for a complex platform that automated cloud services orchestration. This endeavor showcased the power of Node.js for rapid prototyping. I was able to build a fully functional backend and frontend using JavaScript throughout the stack, which significantly accelerated development time. The event-driven, non-blocking I/O model of Node.js proved perfect for handling the multiple, concurrent operations required in cloud orchestration.

What struck me most was how quickly I could assemble a team of senior developers for this project. At that time, finding experienced Node.js developers was easier than sourcing truly skilled senior PHP developers. This abundance of talent, combined with the language consistency across the stack, led to smoother collaboration and faster iteration cycles.

The project's success demonstrated Node.js's capability to handle complex, real-time operations efficiently, from managing service dependencies to scaling resources across multiple cloud providers. This experience not only enhanced my technical skills but also shaped my perspective on choosing technologies for future projects, especially when rapid development and scalability were crucial factors.

Unexpected Opportunities

What I didn't anticipate was how this expertise in Node.js would open doors for me professionally. Several major firms, looking to transition away from their legacy tech stacks, reached out to me for interviews after coming across my work. These companies were actively seeking individuals with proven knowledge in Node.js, which was still a relatively new technology at the time.

These interview opportunities were eye-opening. They revealed a growing trend of established companies recognizing the need to modernize their tech stacks, and Node.js was increasingly seen as a viable solution. The interviews weren't just about technical skills; these firms were interested in my firsthand experience with Node.js in complex, real-world scenarios. My ability to articulate both the technical advantages and potential challenges of adopting Node.js in enterprise environments proved to be a valuable asset. This period marked a significant shift in my career, positioning me as a go-to expert for companies undertaking major technological transitions.

The CTO Opportunity

As my reputation in innovation and tech leadership grew, I was approached by an ambitious FinTech startup with a revolutionary idea: tokenizing real estate loans. This had never been done before, and they were looking for a technical visionary who could turn this concept into reality. The role they were offering? Chief Technology Officer.

Initially, I was both excited and cautious. This wasn't just about leading a team or managing a project; it was about creating something entirely new in the FinTech world. As I delved into the challenge, I realized that my journey - from managing a tech news website in junior high to leading complex projects for international clients - had prepared me for this innovative leap.

The founders were impressed not just by my technical knowledge, but by my ability to envision scalable, cost-effective solutions for unprecedented challenges. I proposed a fully serverless architecture that would ensure near-zero running costs - a critical factor for a B2B company that might spend a significant time demonstrating the infrastructure before generating revenue.

The interview process was intense, involving deep technical discussions about blockchain, real estate finance, and cutting-edge cloud technologies. I found myself drawing on my vast experience with cloud orchestration, serverless architectures, and financial systems. My ability to communicate complex technical concepts clearly and my innovative approach to problem-solving were key factors in securing the position.

This opportunity wasn't just about transitioning existing systems; it was about creating a new technological paradigm in FinTech. It required envisioning a solution that was not only technically sound but also economically viable and scalable for future growth.

Transitioning to the CTO Role

Accepting the CTO position was both exciting and daunting. I was now responsible not just for writing code, but for shaping the entire technological direction of the company. My first few months were a whirlwind of activity:

1. Team Building: I had to build a team almost from scratch. My experience in remote work proved invaluable as we put together a distributed team of talented developers from around the world.
2. Architecture Design: I led the design of our new serverless microservices architecture, drawing heavily on the knowledge I'd gained and documented during my Node.js learning journey.
3. Agile Implementation: We implemented Agile methodologies, adapting them to work for our distributed team. I wrote a series of blog posts about this experience, sharing our successes and failures with the wider tech community.
4. Stakeholder Management: I was working directly with C-level executives and investors. My ability to communicate technical concepts to non-technical audiences, honed through years of blogging, proved crucial.
5. Security and Compliance: Given that we were in the FinTech space, security and regulatory compliance were top priorities. I had to quickly get up to speed on various financial regulations and ensure our systems were robust and secure.

Throughout this transition, I continued to blog, albeit less frequently. My posts now focused more on leadership challenges, architectural decisions, and the intricacies of building a FinTech product. These posts served multiple purposes - they helped me process and reflect on my experiences, provided value to the tech community, and continued to build my personal brand as a technology leader.

Challenges and Growth

The role of CTO brought with it a new set of challenges. I was no longer just responsible for my own work, but for the output and growth of an entire team. Some of the key challenges I faced included:

1. Balancing Technical and Managerial Duties: As someone who loved to code, I found it difficult to step back from day-to-day development. I had to learn to trust my team and focus on higher-level concerns.
2. Scaling the Team and Product: As our product grew in complexity, we had to scale both our team and our infrastructure rapidly. This presented numerous technical and organizational challenges.
3. Navigating the FinTech Landscape: The heavily regulated FinTech industry was new to me. I had to quickly learn about compliance, security protocols, and the specific needs of financial applications.
4. Managing Investor Expectations: Working with investors was a new experience. I had to learn to communicate our technical progress and challenges in a way that non-technical stakeholders could understand and appreciate.

Each of these challenges provided fodder for my blog. I wrote about the difficulties of transitioning from a developer to a leader, the intricacies of scaling a FinTech product, and the lessons I learned about communicating with different stakeholders. These posts resonated with many readers who were on similar journeys or aspiring to leadership roles.

The Power of Transparency

One of the most impactful series of posts I wrote during this time was about a major outage our system experienced. Instead of trying to hide our mistakes, I decided to write a detailed post-mortem, explaining what went wrong, how we fixed it, and what we learned from the experience.

This transparency was initially met with some resistance internally, but it ultimately paid off. Our users appreciated the honesty, it helped rebuild trust after the incident, and it sparked a valuable discussion in the tech community about handling failures and building more resilient systems.

This experience reinforced my belief in the power of sharing not just successes, but also failures and challenges. It demonstrated that vulnerability and honesty could be strengths, not weaknesses, in leadership.

Fractional CTO and Tech Lead: Freelance Freedom

After several years of serving as a full-time CTO, I felt the urge to broaden my horizons and take on new challenges. The tech landscape was evolving rapidly, with emerging fields like AI and blockchain reshaping the industry. I wanted to be at the forefront of these changes, working with a variety of companies and technologies. This led me to transition into the role of a Fractional CTO and Tech Lead, focusing primarily on FinTech and AI ventures.

The Transition to Fractional CTO

The decision to become a Fractional CTO was not made lightly. It meant leaving the security of a full-time position and venturing into the world of freelance consulting. However, the potential benefits were compelling:

1. Diversity of Projects: I could work with multiple companies across different domains, broadening my experience and keeping my skills sharp.
2. Flexibility: I could choose projects that aligned with my interests and values, and have more control over my work-life balance.
3. Continued Learning: Each new project would present unique challenges, forcing me to constantly learn and adapt.
4. Higher Income Potential: By offering specialized, high-level expertise, I could command higher rates than in a traditional full-time role.

Making the Leap

To prepare for this transition, I spent months strategically networking and updating my skills. I drew from my past experiences and lessons learned throughout my career to refine my approach to the fractional CTO role.

I engaged in targeted conversations with key individuals in my network, discussing the concept of fractional CTOs and the value they can bring to both startups and established companies. These discussions were invaluable, allowing me to gain insights from industry peers and potential clients about their needs and expectations.

This focused networking approach helped me to:

1. Proactively identify opportunities for fractional CTO roles
2. Refine my understanding of the market demand for fractional CTO services

3. Identify the most critical skills and knowledge areas to develop further
4. Build relationships with potential clients and collaborators
5. Shape my service offerings to address real pain points in the industry

By leveraging my existing network and reputation, I was able to generate interest and opportunities through word-of-mouth, effectively laying the groundwork for my new role without relying on public announcements or formal marketing efforts.

The First Projects

My first project as a Fractional CTO was with a cybersecurity company. While cybersecurity presented its own unique challenges, I was relieved to find that they were using a serverless stack similar to what I was already familiar with. This common ground provided a solid foundation for me to build upon.

Despite my familiarity with the underlying technology, the project still presented a steep learning curve. I had to quickly immerse myself in the intricacies of cybersecurity, including threat detection, incident response, and security compliance. The serverless architecture, while familiar, needed to be adapted to meet the stringent security requirements of the industry.

This project was an excellent opportunity to apply my existing knowledge of serverless technologies in a new context while rapidly expanding my expertise in cybersecurity. The experience of bridging these two domains - serverless architecture and cybersecurity - proved to be invaluable, opening up new perspectives on how cloud technologies can be leveraged to enhance security measures.

As I navigated this new territory, I found that my ability to quickly grasp and adapt to new concepts, honed through years of diverse tech experiences, was crucial. It allowed me to contribute meaningfully to the project from the start while continually deepening my understanding of cybersecurity principles and practices.

Simultaneously, I took on a Tech Lead role for an AI company developing natural language processing models. This project allowed me to dive deep into the world of machine learning and AI, an area I had long been fascinated by but had limited practical experience with.

Balancing Multiple Projects

One of the biggest challenges of being a Fractional CTO was managing multiple projects simultaneously. Each client had different needs, technologies, and team dynamics. I had to quickly adapt my communication and leadership style to each context.

To manage this complexity, I developed a system:

1. Clear Boundaries: I set clear expectations with each client about my availability and response times.
2. Efficient Communication: I leveraged asynchronous communication tools to stay in touch with teams across different time zones.
3. Knowledge Management: I created a personal wiki to keep track of each project's details, decisions, and progress.
4. Time Blocking: I used time blocking techniques to ensure I was giving adequate focus to each project.

I wrote about these strategies on my blog, sharing my experiences and tips for other freelance CTOs and tech leads. These posts resonated with many readers who were either in similar roles or aspiring to them, further cementing my position as a thought leader in this space.

The AI Revolution

As I continued in my role as a Fractional CTO, I found myself increasingly drawn to AI projects. The rapid advancements in machine learning, particularly in natural language processing and computer vision, were reshaping industries across the board.

I took on several AI-focused projects, including:

1. A healthcare startup using machine learning for early disease detection.
2. An HRTech company using AI to optimize resumes for candidates and adapt them to specific roles.
3. A financial services firm developing AI-powered risk assessment models.

Each of these projects presented unique challenges and learning opportunities. I delved into topics like deep learning, neural network architectures, and ethical AI development. As always, I documented my learnings and insights on my blog.

One of my blog posts that gained significant traction was about Retrieval-Augmented Generation (RAG) systems in the context of enterprise FinTech. The article, titled 'Scalable AI Solutions: Building Cloud-Native RAG Systems for Enterprise FinTech', delved into how this technology is transforming the way financial institutions handle data and generate insights.

In this comprehensive guide, I walked readers through the process of building a cloud-native RAG system specifically designed for FinTech applications. The post covered everything from processing financial documents and generating embeddings to obtaining AI-powered responses, using a stack that included OpenAI, Pinecone, and Flask.

This technical deep-dive not only helped educate my readers about cutting-edge AI applications in finance but also showcased my expertise in combining cloud technologies with AI for practical, industry-specific solutions. The post's popularity demonstrated the high demand for knowledge at the intersection of AI, cloud computing, and FinTech.

As a result of this and similar content, I began receiving inquiries from financial institutions and FinTech startups looking to implement AI solutions, particularly RAG systems, in their operations. This post effectively positioned me as a thought leader in the space of AI applications for FinTech, opening up new opportunities for consulting and leadership roles in this rapidly evolving field.

The Launch of CloudExpat

As I worked on various projects, I noticed a recurring theme: many companies were struggling with cloud optimization. They were either overpaying for resources they didn't need or facing performance issues due to inadequate infrastructure.

Seeing an opportunity, I decided to launch CloudExpat, a startup focused on cloud optimization. This venture allowed me to combine my technical expertise, my experience working with various cloud providers, and my understanding of business needs.

Launching CloudExpat while continuing my work as a Fractional CTO was a significant challenge. I had to balance client work with building and growing my own company. However, the experience was incredibly rewarding. It allowed me to apply all the lessons I had learned over the years – from technical knowledge to team management to product development.

The Power of Personal Branding

Throughout my journey as a Fractional CTO and entrepreneur, my blog continued to play a crucial role in my success. It served as a powerful personal branding tool, showcasing not just my technical skills but also my thought process, problem-solving approach, and leadership philosophy.

Clients often mentioned that they felt like they knew me before we even met, thanks to my blog. This familiarity helped build trust quickly, which was crucial in my role as a fractional CTO where I often had to hit the ground running with new teams.

Moreover, my blog became a lead generation tool. Companies would find my posts when researching solutions to their technical challenges, leading them to reach out for consulting services.

Challenges and Lessons Learned

While the journey as a Fractional CTO and Tech Lead has been rewarding, it hasn't been without its challenges. Some of the key obstacles I've faced include:

1. Balancing Multiple Commitments: Juggling multiple clients, my own startup, and maintaining my blog has been a constant challenge. I've had to become extremely efficient with my time and energy management.
2. Staying Current: The tech world moves at a breakneck pace. Staying up-to-date with the latest developments across multiple domains (FinTech, AI, Cloud Computing) requires constant learning and adaptation.

3. Building Trust Quickly: As a Fractional CTO, I often need to build trust and rapport with new teams rapidly. This requires strong interpersonal skills and the ability to demonstrate value quickly.
4. Navigating Different Company Cultures: Each client has its own unique culture and way of working. Adapting to these different environments while still maintaining my own principles and work style has been a learning experience.
5. Managing Expectations: Clients often have high expectations of what a Fractional CTO can achieve in a limited time. Setting realistic expectations and delivering results within constraints is crucial.

I've written extensively about these challenges on my blog, sharing both my struggles and the strategies I've developed to overcome them. These posts have not only helped me process my experiences but have also provided valuable insights to others in similar roles or considering this career path.

The Impact of AI on Technical Leadership

As AI continues to evolve and reshape industries, its impact on technical leadership roles has been profound. In my work as a Fractional CTO, I've observed and written about several key trends:

1. AI-Driven Decision Making: More companies are leveraging AI to inform strategic decisions. As a technical leader, understanding how to interpret and apply AI-generated insights has become crucial.
2. Ethical AI Development: With the growing influence of AI, ensuring ethical development and deployment of AI systems has become a key responsibility for technical leaders.

3. **AI Integration Challenges:** Many companies struggle with integrating AI into their existing systems and workflows. Guiding this integration process has become a significant part of my role.
4. **Skill Gap Management:** The rapid advancement of AI has created a significant skill gap in many organizations. Part of my role involves developing strategies to upskill existing team members and recruit AI talent.
5. **AI Governance:** Establishing frameworks for AI governance, including data management, model monitoring, and compliance with emerging AI regulations, has become a critical aspect of technical leadership.

These trends and challenges are not just theoretical concepts for me; I've experienced them firsthand in my role as a Fractional CTO. Navigating the complexities of AI integration, addressing ethical concerns, and managing the skill gap have been integral parts of my day-to-day work.

While I haven't yet written a dedicated series on these topics, my experiences have inevitably shaped my perspective and influenced the content I share. The insights I've gained from real-world AI implementation have found their way into various posts, enriching my overall content with practical, hands-on knowledge.

This firsthand experience with AI's impact on technical leadership has not only enhanced my ability to guide companies through AI adoption but has also led to valuable opportunities. It's opened doors to engaging discussions with peers, sparked interesting conversations at industry events, and even influenced some of my client engagements.

The Synergy Between Consulting and Entrepreneurship

Running CloudExpat while working as a Fractional CTO has created an interesting synergy. My consulting work keeps me connected to a variety of industries and challenges, providing insights that inform the development of CloudExpat. Conversely, the hands-on experience of running my own startup enhances my ability to advise other companies as a Fractional CTO.

This dual role has also presented unique content opportunities for my blog. Many posts on my blog explore the delicate balance between consulting, contracting, and entrepreneurship in the tech world. I often delve into what one should know as a business owner versus what's crucial for a tech lead, examining the unique challenges and opportunities that come with wearing multiple hats. These insights, drawn from my experiences navigating these diverse roles, have resonated with a wide audience - from freelance consultants to startup founders. By addressing the intersection of these roles and sharing how lessons from one area apply to others, I've been able to provide content that bridges gaps and offers practical advice for those navigating the multifaceted landscape of tech careers and businesses.

The Role of Content Creation in Professional Growth

Throughout my journey, from junior developer to Fractional CTO and startup founder, content creation has been a constant companion. My blog has evolved alongside my career, reflecting my growing expertise and changing perspectives. It has served multiple crucial functions:

1. Learning Tool: Writing about new technologies and concepts has deepened my understanding and retention of knowledge.
2. Networking Platform: My blog has connected me with like-minded professionals, potential clients, and collaborators from around the world.
3. Personal Brand Builder: Consistent, high-quality content has established me as a thought leader in my areas of expertise.

4. Lead Generation Engine: Many of my consulting opportunities have come directly or indirectly through my blog.
5. Reflection Medium: Blogging has provided a space for me to reflect on my experiences, extract lessons, and plan for the future.

The impact of this consistent content creation on my career cannot be overstated. It has opened doors, created opportunities, and allowed me to build a personal brand that transcends any single job or role.

Looking to the Future

As I look to the future, I see the role of the Fractional CTO evolving further. With the rise of AI, the Internet of Things, and other emerging technologies, the need for experienced technical leaders who can guide companies through digital transformation will only grow.

I plan to continue expanding my skills, taking on challenging projects, and sharing my experiences through my blog. I'm particularly excited about the potential of AI to revolutionize various industries and I aim to be at the forefront of this transformation.

CloudExpat continues to grow, and I'm exploring ways to leverage AI to enhance our cloud optimization solutions. This journey of building a product-based company while continuing my consulting work provides rich material for my blog, allowing me to share insights from both perspectives.

As the tech landscape evolves, so too will the nature of technical leadership. I believe that the ability to adapt, to continuously learn, and to effectively communicate complex ideas will be more important than ever. These are skills I've honed through years of blogging and consulting, and they will undoubtedly serve me well in the years to come.

In conclusion, my journey from a hands-on developer to a Fractional CTO and entrepreneur has been marked by constant learning, adaptation, and growth. Throughout this journey, my commitment to sharing knowledge through my blog has been a key driver of my professional development and success. As I look to the future, I'm excited about the possibilities that lie ahead and grateful for the foundation that technical blogging has provided me.

Reflecting on the Impact of Technical Writing

Looking back on my journey, it's clear that technical writing has been a significant catalyst for my career growth, both directly and indirectly:

1. Direct Impact: Countless times, I've been asked for examples of my work during interviews or client discussions. My blog posts have served as a comprehensive portfolio, showcasing my skills and thought processes.
2. Indirect Impact: Writing about technologies has consistently boosted my confidence in using them. The process of explaining a concept forces you to understand it deeply, often revealing gaps in knowledge that you can then address.
3. Networking: My blog has connected me with like-minded professionals around the world, leading to collaborations, job opportunities, and lasting friendships.
4. Personal Brand: Over time, my consistent writing has helped establish me as a thought leader in certain areas of technology, opening doors to speaking engagements, consulting opportunities, and leadership roles.
5. Continuous Learning: The habit of documenting my learning has kept me accountable to continuous improvement, pushing me to stay ahead of industry trends.

Lessons Learned and Advice for Aspiring Technical Bloggers

As I reflect on my journey, there are several key lessons I'd like to share with aspiring technical bloggers:

1. Start Early: Don't wait until you're an expert to start writing. Document your learning journey from the beginning. Your fresh perspective as a learner can be incredibly valuable to others in the same position.

2. Be Consistent: Regular writing, even if it's not perfect, is better than sporadic bursts of activity. Consistency builds your skills and your audience.

3. Embrace Failures: Some of my most impactful posts have been about challenges I've faced or mistakes I've made. Readers appreciate honesty and learn from others' experiences.

4. Keep Learning: The tech industry moves fast. Make a commitment to continuous learning and share that journey with your readers.

5. Engage with Your Audience: Respond to comments, participate in discussions, and be open to feedback. Building a community around your blog can lead to unexpected opportunities.

6. Write for Yourself First: While it's important to consider your audience, write about topics that genuinely interest you. Your passion will show through in your writing.

7. Quality Over Quantity: While consistent posting is important, never sacrifice quality for the sake of frequency. A well-researched, thoughtful post will have more impact than several rushed, superficial ones.

Conclusion: The Enduring Power of Technical Blogging

As we've traced my journey from a junior high tech enthusiast to a Fractional CTO and entrepreneur, it's clear that technical blogging has been a constant, powerful force in shaping my career. This chapter has illustrated how consistently documenting and sharing my experiences has opened doors, from landing my first job to securing high-level positions and launching my own ventures. The blog has served as a learning tool, a networking platform, and a personal brand builder, demonstrating the multifaceted benefits of technical writing.

My experiences highlight the transformative power of sharing knowledge, not just for career advancement, but for personal growth and community building. Whether it was turning setbacks into valuable content, navigating the transition to leadership roles, or adapting to the challenges of being a Fractional CTO, each step of the journey has reinforced the value of transparent, consistent technical blogging.

As we look ahead to the next chapter, we'll explore how the landscape of technical blogging itself is evolving. In a world of rapid technological advancements, how will the practice of sharing technical knowledge change? What new opportunities and challenges will emerging technologies bring to technical bloggers? By understanding these future trends, we can better prepare ourselves to continue leveraging the power of technical blogging in an ever-changing digital landscape.

CHAPTER 8

The Future of Technical Blogging

The world of technical blogging is changing fast, and we need to keep up. New technologies, different ways people consume content, and shifts in how online platforms work are all shaking things up. In this chapter, we'll look at what's coming down the pike for tech bloggers.

We've got AI starting to write content, questions about who really owns what's posted online, SEO that never stops evolving, and even the potential for VR and AR in blogging. It's a lot to take in, and we'll need to figure out how to use these new tools without losing the human element that makes our writing valuable.

So let's dive in and see how we can stay ahead of the curve, keep innovating, and keep providing real value to our readers in this increasingly complex digital landscape. It's not about predicting the future - it's about being ready for it.

The Future of AI in Blogging

There's no denying that AI is making waves across industries, and blogging is no exception. As we look to the future, AI-driven tools equipped with machine learning and natural language processing capabilities are increasingly being deployed to create content. But what does this mean for the authenticity and depth of our articles? And more crucially, can AI replicate the nuanced experiences and learnings of a developer?

Potential Roles of AI in Future Blogging

- Idea generation
- Dynamic content adaptation
- Interactive code examples
- Automated fact-checking and updates

AI as a Content Creation Aid

AI-driven tools promise the allure of efficiently created content. But it isn't just about churning out articles at scale. These AI tools can:

1. Analyze vast amounts of data to identify trending topics
2. Suggest content structuring that would appeal to a specific audience
3. Help with research by quickly summarizing large volumes of information
4. Assist in generating outlines or first drafts

However, the question remains: can they replace the unique human touch, the subtle nuance, and the experiential wisdom of a seasoned developer?

The Human Element in AI-Assisted Blogging

While AI can be a powerful tool, the heart of blogging is the unique perspective, opinion, and emotion of the writer. These are attributes that no AI, regardless of its sophistication, can truly replicate. Consider the following:

1. Personal Experiences: Only a human can share the joy of cracking a complex coding problem after days of grueling work or the nostalgia of remembering their first computer.
2. Contextual Understanding: Humans can draw connections between seemingly unrelated concepts, bringing a level of creativity that AI currently lacks.
3. Emotional Resonance: The ability to empathize with readers and understand their pain points is a uniquely human trait.
4. Ethical Considerations: Humans can navigate the ethical implications of technology, providing nuanced perspectives that AI might miss.

AI as a Catalyst, Not a Replacement

The essence of AI in the blogging realm can be distilled down to its ability to iterate and augment. While AI suggestions can significantly help in unlocking a writer's block, it's the human touch that breathes life into those suggestions, refining and molding them into impactful narratives.

As we move forward, the key will be to find the right balance, using AI as a tool to enhance our writing process rather than replace it.

This could lead to a new era of blogging where human creativity is amplified by AI capabilities, resulting in content that's both efficient to produce and rich in human insight.

Who Owns the Content?

In an age of aggregation and reposting, the question of content ownership becomes increasingly significant. As bloggers seek to amplify their reach, navigating the line between sharing and ownership will be crucial. It also brings into question the ethics of AI-generated content and its originality.

The Dilemma of Content Aggregation

With platforms that automatically aggregate and repost content, bloggers face a dilemma. The ease of content dissemination is balanced by the risk of lost ownership or attribution. This raises several questions:

1. How do we ensure proper attribution in a world of automated content sharing?
2. What rights do content creators have when their work is aggregated or repurposed?
3. How can bloggers protect their intellectual property while still benefiting from wider distribution?

AI-Generated Content and Ownership

As AI becomes more adept at generating content, the lines of ownership blur further. Who truly owns AI-generated content? The person who prompted the AI? The company that created the AI? Or does it enter the public domain? These are questions that the blogging community, along with legal experts, will need to grapple with in the coming years.

Protecting Work in a Digital World

Protection of intellectual property is a growing concern in our increasingly digital world. However, the solution isn't necessarily stricter digital rights or anti-piracy measures. Instead, we might focus on:

1. Making content so authentic and impactful that any "remix" would pale in comparison to the original.
2. Building a strong personal brand and community around one's work.
3. Strategic sharing across various platforms to ensure a writer's voice remains distinct and recognizable.
4. Using blockchain or other technologies to create immutable records of content creation and ownership.

As we move forward, finding the right balance between protecting our work and allowing for its dissemination will be crucial for technical bloggers.

The SEO Challenge

The realm of Search Engine Optimization is constantly evolving. With algorithm changes and the race to be on the first page, bloggers need to be adept at understanding and adapting to the SEO landscape. But with AI-driven content, can there be a shift in how search engines prioritize content?

The Evolving Nature of SEO

SEO, once an auxiliary part of content creation, has grown to become a pivotal aspect of blogging. As bloggers, understanding ever-evolving algorithms is crucial to ensure content reaches the intended audience. However, the future of SEO is likely to be shaped by several factors:

1. AI and Machine Learning: Search engines are increasingly using AI to understand context and user intent, moving beyond simple keyword matching.
2. Voice Search: With the rise of digital assistants, optimizing for voice search will become increasingly important.
3. User Experience Signals: Factors like page speed, mobile-friendliness, and interactivity are becoming more crucial in search rankings.
4. E-A-T (Expertise, Authoritativeness, Trustworthiness): Google and other search engines are putting more emphasis on the credibility of content creators.

AI-Generated Content and SEO

As AI becomes more prevalent in content creation, it raises questions about how search engines will view and prioritize this content. Will AI-generated content be able to manipulate SEO in unforeseen ways? Or will search engines develop methods to distinguish between human-written and AI-generated content?

It's likely that we'll see a cat-and-mouse game develop, with AI content generation tools trying to create SEO-optimized content, and search engines refining their algorithms to prioritize genuinely valuable, human-centric content.

Quality as the Constant

Despite these changes, one principle remains constant: quality. Whether it's a heartfelt opinion piece, a detailed technical guide, or a unique perspective on a widely discussed topic, high-quality content will always stand out. As long as writers keep pushing their boundaries and stay true to delivering high-caliber content, they'll continue to shine, irrespective of AI's role.

The future of SEO for technical bloggers will likely involve:

1. Focusing on in-depth, authoritative content that demonstrates real expertise
2. Optimizing for user intent rather than just keywords
3. Ensuring technical aspects like site speed and mobile optimization are top-notch
4. Building a strong personal brand and online presence to establish authority
5. Adapting to new forms of search, including voice and visual search

Will AI Overtake All Blogging?

The short answer? No. But it will change the game significantly.

The Rise of AI-Assisted Blogging

AI isn't going to replace bloggers; it's going to create a new breed of "augmented bloggers." Here's what I think this might look like:

1. Idea Generation on Steroids: AI will help bloggers identify trending topics and unexplored niches faster than ever before. Imagine an

AI that can analyze millions of tech discussions in real-time and suggest truly novel blog post ideas.
2. Dynamic Content Adaptation: Future blogs might automatically adjust their content based on the reader's expertise level. A beginner might see more explanations and analogies, while an expert would get a deep dive into advanced concepts – all from the same base article.
3. Interactive Code Examples: AI could power interactive code snippets within blog posts. Readers could modify the code in real-time and see the results, with AI providing instant feedback and suggestions.
4. Automated Fact-Checking and Updates: AI could continuously scan your older posts, suggesting updates when technologies change or new best practices emerge.

The Evolution of the Blogger's Role

As AI takes over more of the grunt work, successful bloggers will need to evolve:

1. Curators of AI Output: Our job will shift towards critically evaluating and refining AI-generated content, ensuring it meets our standards and truly serves our audience.
2. Experience Translators: We'll focus more on interpreting complex concepts through the lens of our real-world experiences – something AI can't replicate.
3. Ethical Tech Advocates: As AI becomes more prevalent in blogging, we'll need to be at the forefront of discussing its ethical implications and setting standards for its use.

The Human Touch: More Valuable Than Ever

In a world of AI-generated content, the authentic human voice will become even more precious. Blogs that maintain a strong personality, share unique insights, and foster genuine community engagement will stand out in the sea of AI-polished content.

As we discussed earlier in this book, Jeff Atwood's "Coding Horror" and Randall Munroe's "XKCD" are prime examples of blogs that AI could never truly replicate or replace. Their unique blend of technical insight, humor, and distinctive perspectives make them virtually impossible for AI to mimic convincingly.

These examples, which we explored in more depth previously, underscore a crucial point: the blogs least likely to be replaced by AI are those with a strong, unique voice and perspective. They don't just convey information; they provide a distinct way of looking at the world that readers connect with on a personal level.

As AI becomes more prevalent in content creation, cultivating this human touch – your unique voice, experiences, and insights – will become more important than ever. It's not just about what information you provide, but how you provide it and the unique perspective you bring to it.

The Bottom Line

AI won't overtake blogging – it'll redefine it. The most successful technical bloggers of the future will be those who learn to dance with AI, leveraging its strengths while doubling down on the irreplaceably human aspects of their craft.

Remember, at its core, great blogging is about connection and trust. And no matter how advanced AI becomes, fostering real connection and earning genuine trust will always be a human endeavor.

The Convergence of Immersive Technologies and Blogging

As the digital world evolves, so do the tools and platforms available to content creators. The rise of AR/VR technologies presents an exciting opportunity for technical bloggers to explore immersive storytelling techniques.

The Potential of Immersive Storytelling

While 3D web experiences like Web3D have been around since the 1990s, they haven't seen widespread adoption in the world of blogging. However, the landscape is changing:

1. Virtual Reality (VR) for Immersive Tutorials: Imagine a VR experience where readers can "step into" a virtual development environment, seeing code structures in 3D space.
2. Augmented Reality (AR) for Real-World Application: AR could allow readers to see how a piece of code or a system architecture would work in their own environment.
3. Mixed Reality for Interactive Learning: Combining real-world and virtual elements could create powerful, interactive learning experiences for complex technical concepts.
4. 360-degree Video for Environmental Context: For topics like IoT or embedded systems, 360-degree video could provide valuable context about the physical environment in which these technologies operate.

AI-Assisted Immersive Content Creation

The creation of immersive content has traditionally required specialized skills. However, the combination of AI and immersive technologies could democratize this process:

1. AI-generated 3D Models: AI could help create 3D models and environments based on text descriptions, making it easier for bloggers to illustrate complex systems or architectures.
2. Automated AR Experiences: AI could assist in creating AR experiences that adapt to the reader's environment, making technical concepts more relatable and applicable.
3. Natural Language Interfaces: AI-powered natural language processing could allow bloggers to create immersive experiences through simple text commands, without needing to learn complex 3D modeling or programming skills.

Challenges and Considerations

While the potential is exciting, there are challenges to consider:

1. Accessibility: Not all readers will have access to VR/AR devices. How can we ensure content remains accessible to all?
2. Content Longevity: As immersive technologies evolve rapidly, how do we ensure our content doesn't become obsolete? This isn't a new challenge in tech. Consider the fate of LaserDiscs or the IBM 3480 tape format. Both were cutting-edge in their time, but now much of their content is nearly inaccessible. How can we create immersive content that remains accessible as technology evolves, avoiding the fate of these abandoned formats? This question becomes crucial as we venture into VR and AR content creation for technical blogging.

3. Balancing Immersion and Information: How do we create immersive experiences that enhance, rather than distract from, the core technical content?
4. Performance and Compatibility: Ensuring smooth performance across various devices and platforms will be crucial for user experience.

Decentralization: A Returning Phenomenon?

The evolution of the digital landscape often resembles a pendulum, swinging between centralization and decentralization. As we look to the future of technical blogging, we see signs of a potential return to more decentralized models.

The Promise of Decentralization

Decentralized platforms offer several potential benefits for technical bloggers:

1. Content Ownership: Greater control over your content and how it's distributed.
2. Censorship Resistance: Reduced risk of having your content removed or suppressed by a central authority.
3. Monetization Options: New models for directly monetizing content without intermediaries.
4. Interoperability: The ability to easily move your content between different platforms and services.

Technologies Driving Decentralization

Several technologies and standards are paving the way for more decentralized content platforms:

1. Blockchain: Providing immutable records of content creation and ownership.
2. IPFS (InterPlanetary File System): A peer-to-peer network for storing and sharing content in a distributed manner.
3. ActivityPub: A decentralized social networking protocol that allows different platforms to interact with each other.
4. Solid: A web decentralization project led by Tim Berners-Lee, aimed at giving users control over their data.

Challenges of Decentralization

While promising, decentralized platforms face several challenges:

1. User Experience: Decentralized systems often lack the polished user experience of centralized platforms.
2. Discovery: Without central algorithms, how do readers discover new content?
3. Scalability: Can decentralized systems handle the load of millions of users and posts?
4. Adoption: Will enough users and creators migrate to these platforms to create viable ecosystems?

The Future: A Hybrid Approach?

Rather than a complete shift to decentralization, we might see a hybrid approach where bloggers leverage both centralized and decentralized platforms. This could involve:

1. Publishing primarily on a decentralized platform but syndicating to centralized platforms for discovery.
2. Using blockchain for content verification and ownership while distributing through traditional channels.
3. Leveraging decentralized storage solutions while maintaining a centralized front-end for better user experience.

As technical bloggers, staying informed about these developments and experimenting with decentralized technologies could open up new opportunities for content creation, distribution, and monetization.

Long-form Content in a Bite-sized World

As attention spans shrink and the demand for bite-sized content grows, one might question the future of long-form content. Yet, the thirst for in-depth, comprehensive content remains, especially in the technical blogging sphere. The challenge lies in presenting it in an engaging and accessible manner.

The Enduring Value of Long-form Content

Despite the trend towards shorter content, long-form articles continue to provide unique value:

1. Depth of Analysis: Complex technical topics often require extensive explanation and context.

2. SEO Benefits: Search engines tend to favor longer, more comprehensive content.
3. Authority Building: In-depth articles demonstrate expertise and build trust with readers.
4. Problem Solving: Detailed guides and tutorials can provide complete solutions to complex issues.

Strategies for Long-form Content in the Future

To keep long-form content relevant and engaging, we might see the following strategies emerge:

1. Modular Content: Breaking down long articles into interconnected, bite-sized modules that can be consumed individually or as a whole.
2. Progressive Disclosure: Using expandable sections or "read more" links to allow readers to dive deeper into specific areas of interest.
3. Multi-media Integration: Incorporating video, interactive diagrams, and audio elements to break up text and cater to different learning styles.
4. Adaptive Content: Using AI to personalize the depth and focus of content based on the reader's expertise level and interests.
5. Social Proof and Engagement: Integrating social sharing and commenting features throughout the article to maintain engagement.

Navigating the Future Landscape of Content Creation Tools

As AI continues to evolve, the landscape of writing aids will undoubtedly expand. Writers, especially those just starting, should remain agile and open to these advancements. Yet, it's crucial to approach these tools as companions rather than crutches.

Emerging Content Creation Tools

1. AI Writing Assistants: Tools like GPT-3 based platforms that can help generate ideas, outlines, or even draft sections of articles.
2. Advanced Grammar and Style Checkers: Going beyond basic grammar to suggest improvements in clarity, tone, and engagement.
3. SEO Optimization Tools: AI-powered tools that provide real-time suggestions for improving search engine visibility.
4. Content Personalization Engines: Tools that help tailor content for different audience segments or platforms.
5. Collaborative Writing Platforms: Advanced tools that facilitate real-time collaboration and version control for team-based content creation.

Balancing Tool Usage with Authenticity

While these tools can enhance efficiency and quality, it's vital to maintain the authenticity and unique voice that readers value. Here are some guidelines for navigating this landscape:

1. Use tools to augment, not replace your writing process.
2. Always review and refine AI-generated content to ensure it aligns with your voice and expertise.

3. Prioritize your unique insights and experiences – that's what sets your content apart.
4. Stay informed about the capabilities and limitations of the tools you use.
5. Be transparent with your audience about your use of AI and other advanced tools.

Conclusion: Embracing the Future of Technical Blogging

As we look towards the horizon of technical blogging, we see a landscape rich with both challenges and opportunities. The convergence of AI, immersive technologies, and decentralized platforms promises to reshape how we create, distribute, and consume content. Yet, amidst this technological revolution, the core essence of blogging remains unchanged – the sharing of knowledge, experiences, and insights.

Key takeaways for navigating the future of technical blogging:

1. Embrace AI as a Tool, Not a Replacement: Use AI to enhance your writing process, but remember that your unique voice and experiences are irreplaceable.
2. Adapt to New Content Formats: Explore immersive and interactive content formats, but always prioritize accessibility and user experience.
3. Stay Informed About Decentralization: Keep an eye on decentralized platforms and technologies, as they may offer new opportunities for content ownership and distribution.

4. Balance Depth with Accessibility: Continue to create in-depth content, but explore new ways to make it digestible and engaging for your audience.
5. Remain Agile with Tools: Stay open to new content creation tools, but use them judiciously to maintain your authentic voice.
6. Focus on Quality and Authenticity: Regardless of technological changes, high-quality, authentic content will always be valuable.
7. Continuous Learning: The landscape is evolving rapidly – make continuous learning a priority to stay ahead of the curve.

As technical bloggers, we stand at the forefront of these changes. By embracing new technologies while staying true to our passion for sharing knowledge, we can shape the future of technical communication. The journey ahead is exciting, challenging, and full of potential. Let's step into this future with curiosity, creativity, and a commitment to excellence in our craft.

Remember, at its core, technical blogging is about connecting people with knowledge. As long as we keep this mission at the heart of our efforts, we'll continue to thrive, regardless of how the technological landscape shifts around us.

FINAL THOUGHTS

The Blog That Stood the Test of Time

Looking back at my journey through the tech industry, it's clear that one thing has remained constant: my blog. Coincidentally, this digital space I created years ago has become more than just a collection of posts; it's a testament to my growth in the field.

As a result of maintaining this blog, I've had the opportunity to document my experiences, from debugging complex issues to implementing cutting-edge technologies. Be that as it may, the true value of this platform extends beyond mere documentation.

One particularly impactful blog post I wrote addressed a common challenge in Node.js deployment: packaging scripts into standalone binaries. Born from my experience with SQS message processing on EC2 instances, I wrote about using 'pkg' to bundle Node.js applications into single executables. This solution eliminated dependency issues and dramatically reduced deployment times in cloud environments. The post resonated widely, offering a practical alternative to rewriting Node.js scripts in compiled languages like Go. It became a go-to reference in my network for developers grappling with Node.js deployment in time-sensitive scenarios, demonstrating how sharing solutions to real-world problems can provide lasting value to the tech community.

Throughout my career, I've transitioned between various roles and technologies. The blog has served as a record of these changes, capturing the evolution of my skills and knowledge. From my early days wrestling with jQuery and PHP, to diving deep into AngularJS, and later exploring the world of Node.js, Typescript, Go, and Serverless Architectures, each technological shift is chronicled in my posts.

Baring in mind the rapid pace of technological advancement, having a stable platform to return to has been invaluable. It's interesting to revisit old posts and see how certain predictions played out, or how solutions to problems have evolved over time. For instance, a post I wrote about optimizing database queries in 2010 seems almost quaint now, given the advancements in cloud capabilities and the cost of running a database instance.

The blog has also played a significant role in my career progression. As I moved from developer to tech lead, and eventually to CTO, my writing reflected this growth. The technical jargon that once dominated my posts gradually gave way to more accessible explanations, mirroring my own journey in learning to communicate complex concepts to diverse audiences.

Networking and community building have been unexpected benefits of maintaining this blog. The connections made through comments, emails, and even at conferences where people recognized my work have been invaluable. These interactions have led to collaborations, job opportunities, and friendships that extend beyond the digital realm.

One particularly significant outcome came from a blog post I wrote about implementing a custom authentication system. After publishing the post, I attended a local tech meetup where I met a developer who had implemented a similar system. Through our discussion and their valuable feedback, I was inspired to take on a pioneering project: one of the first (if not the first) implementations of OAuth authentication using purely serverless technologies. This innovative approach not only solved a complex problem in the serverless ecosystem but also garnered significant attention in the developer community, further establishing my expertise in cutting-edge authentication solutions and serverless architectures.

Looking ahead, the blog will undoubtedly continue to evolve, much like the technology landscape it covers. There's still much to explore, from emerging AI technologies to the next generation of web development frameworks. I'm particularly excited about the potential of edge computing and its impact on application architecture. Whatever comes next, this platform will be there to capture the journey.

In conclusion, while technologies have come and gone, and my roles have changed, this blog has remained a constant. It's been a place to share knowledge, connect with others, and chart my own growth. For those considering starting their own blog, the benefits extend far beyond the written word. It's a journey of continuous learning and connection, one that I'm grateful to have embarked upon.

As I look to the future, I can't help but feel a sense of anticipation. The tech industry is never static, and neither is this blog. There will always be new challenges to tackle, new technologies to explore, and new insights to share. And through it all, this blog will continue to be my digital home, a place where ideas are born, experiences are shared, and a community comes together.

Glossary

A

Agile: A project management and product development approach that emphasizes flexibility, customer collaboration, and rapid iteration.

AI (Artificial Intelligence): The simulation of human intelligence in machines programmed to think and learn like humans.

AngularJS: A JavaScript-based open-source front-end web application framework.

API (Application Programming Interface): A set of protocols and tools for building software applications.

AR (Augmented Reality): An interactive experience where the real-world environment is enhanced with computer-generated information.

B

Binary Code: A method of representing text or computer processor instructions using the binary number system's two binary digits, 0 and 1.

Blockchain: A decentralized, distributed ledger technology that records transactions across many computers.

Blog: A regularly updated website or web page, typically run by an individual or small group, written in an informal or conversational style.

C

Cloud Computing: The delivery of computing services over the internet, including servers, storage, databases, networking, software, and analytics.

CMS (Content Management System): Software that helps users create, manage, and modify content on a website without needing specialized technical knowledge.

Content Marketing: A strategic marketing approach focused on creating and distributing valuable, relevant, and consistent content to attract and retain a clearly defined audience.

CTO (Chief Technology Officer): An executive-level position focused on scientific and technological issues within an organization.

D

Decentralization: The process of distributing or dispersing functions, powers, people, or things away from a central location or authority.

DevOps: A set of practices that combines software development (Dev) and IT operations (Ops) to shorten the systems development life cycle while delivering features, fixes, and updates frequently in close alignment with business objectives.

Django: A high-level Python web framework that encourages rapid development and clean, pragmatic design.

E

E-A-T (Expertise, Authoritativeness, Trustworthiness): A concept in SEO that refers to the factors Google uses to evaluate content quality.

Emacs: An extensible, customizable, free/libre text editor.

F

FinTech: Financial technology, referring to new tech that seeks to improve and automate the delivery and use of financial services.

Full Stack Developer: A developer who can work on both the front-end and back-end portions of an application.

G

Git: A distributed version-control system for tracking changes in source code during software development.

GitHub: A web-based hosting service for version control using Git.

Go (Golang): An open-source programming language developed by Google.

Google Cloud Platform (GCP): A suite of cloud computing services offered by Google that runs on the same infrastructure that Google uses internally for its end-user products.

H

HTML: Hypertext Markup Language, the standard markup language for documents designed to be displayed in a web browser.

I

IPFS (InterPlanetary File System): A protocol and peer-to-peer network for storing and sharing data in a distributed file system.

J

JavaScript: A high-level, interpreted programming language that is a core technology of the World Wide Web.

Jekyll: A simple, blog-aware, static site generator for personal, project, or organization sites.

K

Kotlin: A cross-platform, statically typed, general-purpose programming language with type inference.

L

Linux: A family of open-source Unix-like operating systems based on the Linux kernel.

M

Machine Learning: A subset of artificial intelligence that provides systems the ability to automatically learn and improve from experience without being explicitly programmed.

Markdown: A lightweight markup language with plain text formatting syntax. It is used to format readme files, for writing messages in online discussion forums, and to create rich text using a plain text editor.

MEAN Stack: A JavaScript software stack for building dynamic web sites and web applications, consisting of MongoDB, Express.js, AngularJS, and Node.js.

Microservices: A software development technique that structures an application as a collection of loosely coupled services.

N

Node.js: An open-source, cross-platform, JavaScript runtime environment that executes JavaScript code outside of a web browser.

NLP (Natural Language Processing): A subfield of linguistics, computer science, and artificial intelligence concerned with the interactions between computers and human language.

O

OAuth: An open standard for access delegation, commonly used as a way for internet users to grant websites or applications access to their information on other websites but without giving them the passwords.

Open Source: A type of computer software in which source code is released under a license in which the copyright holder grants users the rights to use, study, change, and distribute the software to anyone and for any purpose.

Orgmode: A major mode for GNU Emacs, a plain text system for note-taking and project planning.

P

PHP: A popular general-purpose scripting language especially suited to web development.

Python: An interpreted, high-level, general-purpose programming language.

R

React: A JavaScript library for building user interfaces.

RegTech: Regulatory technology, a new field within the financial services industry that utilizes information technology to enhance regulatory processes.

Ruby on Rails: A server-side web application framework written in Ruby.

S

SEO (Search Engine Optimization): The process of improving the quality and quantity of website traffic to a website or a web page from search engines.

Serverless Computing: A cloud computing execution model in which the cloud provider runs the server, and dynamically manages the allocation of machine resources.

Spacemacs: A community-driven Emacs distribution that aims to combine the best features of Emacs and Vim.

Static Site Generator: A tool that generates a full static HTML website based on raw data and a set of templates.

T

TypeScript: A programming language developed and maintained by Microsoft, which is a strict syntactical superset of JavaScript and adds optional static typing to the language.

U

UX (User Experience): The overall experience of a person using a product such as a website or computer application, especially in terms of how easy or pleasing it is to use.

V

Version Control: The management of changes to documents, computer programs, large web sites, and other collections of information.

VR (Virtual Reality): A simulated experience that can be similar to or completely different from the real world.

W

WordPress: A free and open-source content management system based on PHP and MySQL.

X

XML: Extensible Markup Language, a markup language that defines a set of rules for encoding documents in a format that is both human-readable and machine-readable.

Y

Y Combinator's HackerNews: a popular social news website and community created by Y Combinator, a San Francisco-based startup accelerator, where users share and discuss articles, primarily related to technology, startups, and entrepreneurship.

www.ingramcontent.com/pod-product-compliance
Lightning Source LLC
Chambersburg PA
CBHW071051240526
45471CB00015B/1641